IMPROVING THE VILLAGE

IMPROVING THE VILLAGE

STOCKBRIDGE, MASSACHUSETTS, AND THE LAUREL HILL ASSOCIATION

KIRIN JOYA MAKKER
AND SARAH ALLABACK

LIBRARY OF AMERICAN LANDSCAPE HISTORY

AMHERST, MASSACHUSETTS

For my parents, Donna and Sudesh

Library of American Landscape History
P.O. Box 1323
Amherst, MA 01004
www.lalh.org

Library of Congress Control Number: 2024946407
ISBN: 978-1-952620-42-3

Designed by Jonathan D. Lippincott
Set in Granjon

Distributed by
National Book Network
nbnbooks.com

Frontispiece: Lake Mahkeenac, view from Shadow Brook, 1899. Digital Commonwealth.

CONTENTS

PREFACE

Focusing on the bucolic Berkshire town of Stockbridge, *Improving the Village* provides a keystone study for a comprehensive understanding of America's village improvement movement. Stockbridge was home to the nation's first such organization, the Laurel Hill Association, which flourished and became a model for village improvement societies throughout America. That the Laurel Hill Association has continued to guide stewardship of the town into the twenty-first century makes its story especially significant.

The particulars of the town's early history proved fascinating, involving as they do the first missionaries in the region—including the brilliant preacher Jonathan Edwards—Mohicans, freed slaves, and literary-minded settlers. A deep sense of these connections inspired village reformers to protect and improve their town as it grew and was threatened by development. The story of the Laurel Hill Association resonates today in the local community-minded volunteer groups that have formed in towns and urban neighborhoods throughout the country.

LALH was fortunate in pairing Kirin Makker of Hobart and William Smith Colleges with our senior manuscript editor, Sarah Allaback, who is also an authority on nineteenth-century women writers. Their combined talents as historians and authors have produced an engaging book, illustrated with many never-before-published archival images, offering new perspectives on colonial settlement, the cultural history of an exceptionally beautiful New England town, and the development of the village improvement movement in America. I am grateful to both of them for the years of research and writing, and to Daniel J. Nadenicek, former dean, University of Georgia, for his early guidance of the project.

My thanks also go to Carol Betsch, who edited the text and developed the extensive illustration program; Jonathan Lippincott for the book's deft design; and Mary Bellino for her keen editorial eye and superb index. I am also grateful to the funders who generously underwrote the years-long effort, especially Susan L. Klaus, whose initial gift launched the initiative, Nancy Carol Carter, Frank Garretson, and Sally and Fred Harris. My thanks also go to the donors to the Nancy R. Turner Fund and the Ann Douglass Wilhite Fund, who made finishing the work possible. Thanks are also due to the board of directors of Library of American Landscape History for their enduring support of the LALH publishing program and its mission to educate broad audiences about American landscape history.

Robin Karson, Hon. ASLA
Executive Director

INTRODUCTION

The history of Stockbridge, Massachusetts, and its role as a leader in civic improvement begins along the Housatonic River in the fertile plain surrounded by the Berkshire Hills. First discovered by Indigenous peoples, the Valley of the Housatonic became known for its beauty long before European settlers set foot on the land. Populated by unexpected lakes, bogs, and riverlets and seasonally adorned with meadows, it was a dramatic landscape that would inspire legends, poems, and novels as well as such honorifics as "the American Lake District" and "the Piedmont of America."

The area's early colonial settlement as a Christian mission determined the shape of its future village. By the 1730s, a mission house, school building, and meetinghouse stood on the plain, along with the homes of four founding families and Mohican shelters. The leader of the mission, Reverend John Sergeant, soon chose to symbolize his status by moving up to Prospect Hill, the future site of great estates. From this vantage a picturesque scene unfolded, with the settlement in the foreground surrounded by meadows, the meandering river, and Beartown, Monument, and Stockbridge Mountains in the distance.[1]

By the mid-nineteenth century, Stockbridge was an oasis amid villages destined to become locations for industry—West Stockbridge, where the Williams River powered mills, and Richmond to the northwest. Natural twists and turns in the Housatonic prevented any major industrial development within the village boundaries. Over time, the primary businesses—including a tavern, bank, and post office—and prominent houses stood along a broad, tree-lined main street, the "great road" from Boston to Albany, bisected by a north–south county road.[2] The closest city was Pittsfield, about twelve miles north.

"Monument Mountain, Stockbridge (looking across Flooded Fields, Great Barrington)," 1899. Photo by Arthur Wentworth Scott from John Coleman Adams, *Nature Studies in Berkshire*. The Clark Digital Collections.

The New England town was home to an unusual concentration of authors, highly educated civic leaders, ministers, and lawyers—many of them graduates of Yale and nearby Williams College. Residents had access to stagecoach travel to New York and Boston, and, beginning in 1850, regular rail service. Many villagers were sophisticated readers and travelers who closely followed the work of novelists and poets such as Nathaniel Hawthorne and William Cullen Bryant and the art of Hudson River School painters, architects, and landscape gardeners, as well as recent technological advancements in farming and sanitation.

In 1853, Mary Hopkins (later Goodrich) founded the nation's first village beautification society—the Laurel Hill Association, named for a landscape preserved by the prominent Sedgwick family and made famous by the internationally renowned author Catharine Maria Sedgwick. The state-authorized volunteer organization embraced emerging notions of cultural and civic improvement and charged itself with maintaining public spaces throughout the Berkshire village, in particular guiding tree planting and maintenance of burial grounds. Hopkins and her cohort soon discovered that countless villages across the country shared their desire for civic betterment. By 1880, "Old Stockbridge-on-the-Plain" was "known everywhere as the model village of New England."[3]

The 1893 World's Columbian Exposition displayed the ideal of the "city beautiful" to the world and kindled the national zeal for civic betterment. Mira Lloyd Dock of Harrisburg, Pennsylvania, and Jessie M. Good in Springfield, Ohio, spearheaded efforts dedicated to local and national improvement. Both women recognized Mary Hopkins Goodrich as the pioneering force behind their "modern" movement. The founder of the Laurel Hill Association had taken on the civic responsibility of keeping streets and water sources free of garbage—issues that they were now addressing in the battle to conquer malaria and increase public support for sanitation boards. Goodrich's efforts led to the founding of hundreds of village improvement associations based on the Stockbridge model.

Throughout generations of growth and change, the Laurel Hill Association has remained a consistent factor in the life of Stockbridge, continuing the tradition of holding annual meetings, supporting community enhancement projects, and maintaining public landscapes. This is the story of how the Laurel Hill Association became the exemplar in a national effort to inspire volunteer community maintenance and land stewardship—legacies that continue to enrich the American landscape.

IMPROVING THE VILLAGE

Old Mission House, Stockbridge, c. 1900–1915. Library of Congress Prints and Photographs Division.

ONE

A MISSION IN WESTERN MASSACHUSETTS

In the winter of 1852, Electa Fidelia Jones completed *Stockbridge, Past and Present; or, Records of an Old Mission Station,* a history of her hometown from its earliest settlement by the Mohican tribe to its status as a popular resort. Jones was known as the village genealogist, but this was the fifty-two-year-old's first effort to write a book.[1] Motivated by Stockbridge's increasing fame as a tourist destination, she set out to correct published mistakes related to local sites, contribute to the rising interest in people and places, and more adequately accommodate visitors by improving "the office of cicerone." Her work would feed the "genealogical mania" sweeping through the Berkshire region. Previous efforts to supply the public with an adequate local history, such as *The History of Berkshire* (1829), not only were outdated but failed to adequately chronicle the village's history as a Christian mission. Now that Stockbridge was "the theme of the poet, the painter or the traveler, and the shrine of even the pilgrim," Jones's "records" would add to the romance of the region with historical facts worthy of fiction.[2]

During her research, Jones came upon a rare "History" she attributed to Captain Hendrick Aupaumut, the first Indigenous historian to use writing, rather than narration handed down through generations, to record his people's past.[3] A third-generation Christian, Aupaumut was born in Stockbridge around 1757 and educated in the mission school.[4] He served as a Christian missionary and interpreter, facilitating dialogue between the Indigenous people, the new settlers, and the Dutch. His account began with his earliest ancestors, who were driven by famine from a distant continent and explored the new land in search of a great river, "flowing and ebbing" like their native Muh-he-con-nuk. They discovered the Hudson Valley, a region of life-giving water and plentiful game.[5]

3

In later years, pressure from Dutch settlers led "the people of the continually flowing waters" to settle along the Housatonic.[6]

As she read his account, Jones visualized the noble historian and peacemaker. The beautiful landscape Aupaumut described represented a physical Eden, and, as a Christian, he took part in realizing God's spiritual plan. Although the Mohican tribe had long since relocated, members returned to their homeland every few years. The ten pages of Aupaumut's poetic prose she transcribed into her book spoke to her own Christian values and the universal brotherhood of believers. She aspired to show that the Mohicans "still have a national existence, still hold the religion which they learned upon this spot, and still love, with true Indian fervor, the homes and the graves of their fathers" in Stockbridge.[7]

Now that only a few descendants of the tribe remained, the Mohicans who had "melted away" lived on in oral history and on Laurel Hill, the idyllic landscape that Catharine Maria Sedgwick had made "a classic ground."[8] Sedgwick's popular novel *Hope Leslie; or Early Times in the Massachusetts* chronicled the relationship between colonists and the Indians they encountered. Curious readers often visited Stockbridge, some even traveling from abroad to meet the author and explore the landscape she described. Jones trusted that her nonfiction account of the town would serve as an appropriate guide during their stay. More than half her book was dedicated to an intricate retelling of the region's early history and the story of the Christian mission determined to colonize a distant corner of Massachusetts. After immersing herself in Aupaumut's writings, Jones turned to an earlier manuscript, *Historical Memoirs, Relating to the Housatunnuk Indians: or, An Account of the Methods used, and Pains taken, for the Propagation of the Gospel among that heathenish Tribe, and the Success thereof, under the Ministry of the late Reverend Mr. John Sergeant* by Samuel Hopkins, to inform her understanding of the colonizer's perspective. A Yale College graduate and part of a network of powerful New England ministers, Hopkins was considered "provider and historian" of the missionary endeavor.[9]

The founding of Stockbridge appears to have been a collaborative venture, with the Mohicans taking the lead, if only because their options were so limited.[10] As settlers ventured further westward, the tribe felt increasing pressure to plan for its future. When a group of New Englanders petitioned for a tract of Mohican land in 1722, Chief Konkapot and his community saw an opportunity to create an alliance, of sorts. Hopkins and fellow ministers agreed that the Housatonic Indians were not only likely candidates for a Christian mission but potentially useful allies against the French. To further their effort, Hopkins arranged for William Williams, the pastor at Hatfield, to appeal to the Commission of Indian Affairs in Boston, of which Governor Belcher was a board member. Hopkins's push to establish a Christian mission conveniently coincided with an upcoming meeting in Springfield, where Konkapot and Umpachenee, veterans of war, were to be granted military titles. At the ceremony, state officials announced their plan for a Stockbridge mission.[11]

In 1724, Konkapot and twenty other Mohicans sold the desired land—the future site of the towns of Sheffield, Great Barrington, Egremont, and Mount Washington, as well as parts of Alford, Stockbridge, and West Stockbridge—to a group of fifty-five settlers in the County of Hampshire. The property lines avoided two Mohican communities separated by about ten miles: Ska-te-hook, home of the Mohican sachem Umpachenee, and the Great Meadow (Wnahtukook), where Konkapot's cabin stood on a knoll north of a brook. One of Konkapot's friends, Jehoiakim Van Valkenburgh, who served as his interpreter, lived nearby at the west end of Wnahtukook, along with a few other Dutch families.

Over the next decade, as these groups intermingled, Konkapot expressed interest in accepting the Christian faith.[12] His potential willingness to adopt a foreign religion occurred at a time when the Boston commissioners were concerned about their unstable western border, a region in which Catholic French Canadians threatened to gain a foothold. Since the aftermath of King Philip's War, two generations earlier, tribes like the Mohicans were considered potential allies—especially in their ability to shore up alliances among one another and to resist the French. The Mohicans had long fostered relationships with western tribes, including the Miami, Delaware, and Shawnee, which made their allegiance in the war particularly beneficial to the English.[13]

During the summer of 1734, the Reverends Williams and [Nehemiah] Bull traveled to Housatonic and lodged with members of the community. The Mohicans conferred among themselves and associated tribes for four days before agreeing to welcome a missionary to their lands. Shortly after their conference, the Boston commissioners secured funds for John Sergeant, a graduate of Yale College, to direct the mission, and in the fall of 1734, he set out from Westfield on an exploratory visit to the distant outpost some forty miles west.[14] Travel had improved somewhat with the arrival of the settlers, who had incorporated the nearby town of Sheffield the year before, and Sergeant knew of a house along the road that served as a hostel for travelers. But he described his route as "thro' a most doleful wilderness" along "the worst road, perhaps, that ever was rid," and having misjudged the distance, he spent a night in the wilderness without food or shelter.[15] It was the first of many experiences that would test the young missionary's fitness for his calling.

By November, Sergeant was preaching and teaching from a new building in the settlement soon incorporated as Great Barrington. His tutoring responsibilities required him to return to Yale, but he did so in the company of Konkapot and Umpachenee's sons, nine-year-old Nungkawwat and eight-year-old Etowaukaum.[16] Their fathers realized the importance of cultivating the settlers as allies and understood that learning the English language and culture was increasingly crucial to survival. For the Housatonic Indians, who had long practiced such social exchanges as a way of reinforcing ties with other tribes, this cultural exchange signaled the beginning of the commitment to fulfill their version of the mission.

In the course of shoring up a mutual alliance, the New Englanders and the Mohicans traveled back and forth between the western Massachusetts settlement and Westfield, Springfield, Deerfield, and New Haven, seventy-five miles distant, often meeting government officials from Boston at these towns. Such meetings not only established meaningful relationships between the players but also created a new map of the landscape, connecting the settlement of the Berkshire Hills to New England's elite centers of learning. Further cultural exchanges took place during the week before Sergeant's ordination in August 1735, which had been planned to coincide with Governor Belcher's signing of a treaty with several tribes in Deerfield.[17] In addition to government officials and other English representatives, the audience included a large contingent of Mohicans, who sat to one side, rising as a group to signal their affirmation when Sergeant was formally ordained. Within two months after returning to Stockbridge, Sergeant had performed over forty baptisms.[18]

The following spring, government representatives began fulfilling one of the governor's promises to the Housatonic Indians by reorganizing the land arrangement to accommodate their seasonal schedule. The Mohicans traditionally spent the summer cultivating land in the Great Meadow, access to which had been compromised by the original land grant.[19] To facilitate its plan, the Massachusetts legislature authorized construction of a new "township 6 miles square to be laid out on the Housatonic River immediately north of Monument Mountain." This area included the fertile soil in the village, where the sachem lived, and required "the proprietors and settlers" of the Upper Housatonic to give up portions of land. One sixtieth of the tract was set aside for Sergeant, Timothy Woodbridge, and four English families, who would be introduced as "civilizing factors." Woodbridge boarded with Konkapot before building the first permanent English-style house in "Indian Town" in 1736. The next year Sergeant, who had been staying in Great Barrington, built his own house on the plain.[20] The state legislature offered funds for a forty-by-thirty-foot meetinghouse and a school building.[21]

Electa Jones's book included the genealogy of the four founding families of Stockbridge, headed by Ephraim Williams Sr., Josiah Jones, Ephraim Brown, and Joseph Woodbridge, brother of Timothy. Later accounts of the founding story emphasized the selection of families descending from the Puritans and reflecting "the highest respectability and the best character." This auspicious beginning offered more promise than previous settlements launched by companies of speculators, particularly since it involved removing the typical "doubtful characters who inevitably inhabited the fringes of such settlements."[22]

In May 1739, "Indian Town" was christened "Stockbridge" after the eponymous town in Hampshire, England, founded in the thirteenth century. The two villages shared similar landscape characteristics; both were settled on level ground along a river and organized around a major east–west road.[23] The Indigenous residents soon became known as the "Stockbridge Indians." Governance of the community was at least partially shared between the two founding cultures. At the first town meeting, one Englishman and two Mohicans, John Konkapot and Aaron Umpachenee, were chosen as selectmen.[24] As they celebrated the new township, the settlers were encouraged by Sergeant's marriage to Abigail Williams, the daughter of Ephraim Williams Sr. Sergeant built her a new house, in the popular Georgian style, on the hill overlooking the village plain. The first Congregational church, a two-story wood-frame building with two aisles, was dedicated on Thanksgiving Day, 1739. The next year, the Sergeants had a daughter, Electa.[25]

By this time, Sergeant could communicate in the Mohican language and, with Timothy Woodbridge as schoolmaster, taught the Indians and began translating the Bible for them. The campaign for Indian education influenced Col. Ephraim Williams Jr., who included an annual sum dedicated to instructing the Stockbridge Indians in "Christian Knowledge" as part of his first will.[26] Although Sergeant's vision for developing the mission was left unfulfilled— he died in 1749 at age thirty-seven—the missionary would be remembered for securing the friendship of the Indians.[27]

The search for a new minister ended in 1751, when the charismatic preacher Jonathan Edwards accepted leadership of the mission.[28] Edwards, with his wife Sarah and their eight children, moved into John Sergeant's first house, eventually building an extension to accommodate the large family. The decision to live within the community, rather than look down on it from Prospect Hill, eased the family's transition to mission life. Living in the remote wilderness no doubt reduced Edwards's daily tasks as a pastor, allowing time to muse on theological topics and to delve into the origins of the religious tenets so integral to his mind and soul. Edwards had recently broken with his parish fifty miles to the east in Northampton over theological disagreements, but his skills as "scholar and preacher" were still much admired. Arguably the nation's first celebrity preacher, Edwards had helped inspire the Great Awakening with his passionate oratorical style and flair for writing.[29]

At the Mission House, sequestered in a four-by-six-foot "closet" within a front room facing the main street, Edwards composed some of the most influential writings in American history.[30] In 1754, the year the French and Indian War began, he published his treatise *The Freedom of the Will,* and his two famous dissertations followed.[31] In 1757, Edwards grudgingly accepted the presidency of Princeton (after the death of his son-in-law Aaron Burr) and died of fever there within a few months. The writings he left behind, among the most esteemed of his profession to this day, would become part of the cultural legacy of the Berkshires.[32]

During the period between Edwards's departure and the arrival of a new minister, the French and Indian War ostensibly ended with the fall of Quebec. This victory cleared the way for future colonists, and in 1759 a thousand English families moved into the region, seeking inexpensive land in a "wilderness" that now seemed civilized. Within two years, this rush of residents resulted in the establishment of Berkshire County, the last such jurisdiction to be created in Massachusetts. The settlers' cause was aided by Elijah Williams, Ephraim Jr.'s half-brother, a lawyer and town official intent on acquiring Indian land. West Stockbridge would grow around the Williams Iron Works. Located on the Williams River, a branch of the Housatonic, the new village took advantage of a series of smaller tributaries by building dams to power a variety of industries. Forty families, from towns as distant as Sturbridge, seventy-five miles to the east, and Farmington, Connecticut, had settled in the region by 1774, when the town of West Stockbridge incorporated.[33]

Despite their remote location, Stockbridge residents learned about the battle of Lexington by noon on Friday, April 19, less than two days after the event.[34] William Goodrich and Daniel Nimham, a Munsee Lenape sachem who had joined Mohican kin, were among the New Englanders who led Stockbridge's minutemen. After the surrender at Saratoga, townspeople recalled defeated British troops and Hessians passing through the town. Aupaumut served in a company of volunteers and assumed the title of captain at King's Bridge, New York.[35] The Indigenous participants were later singled out by George Washington, who arranged for a West Point contingent to provide a feast featuring an eleven-hundred-pound ox roasted whole. The Stockbridge Indians' loyalty throughout the wars was ingrained in the town's history.[36]

During wartime, Silas and Anna Bingham had opened a store across the street from the inn and catered to soldiers passing through on the way to Fort Ticonderoga. Advertisements for Bingham's Tavern, the core of today's Red Lion Inn, first appeared in local papers in 1778. After Silas's death in 1781, Anna successfully petitioned the General Court in Boston to renew their license and went on to run the inn for the next eleven years. She fought hard to keep her property and became the first woman "litigate" to appeal to the U.S. Supreme

Court, leaving an imprint on her community as a leading entrepreneur. Her inn would become the most prominent business in town.[37]

In the mid-1780s, the majority of the Stockbridge Indians resettled in New Stockbridge, New York, near Oneida Lake, the beginning of decades of transience as the tribe was "removed" to make room for white settlers.[38] John Sergeant Jr., who had served as minister to the Indians since 1775, arranged to spend six months of the year living with them. He maintained this pattern until 1796, when he relocated his family to the settlement in New Stockbridge.[39]

View on the Housatonic, Pittsfield, c. 1905–1915. Library of Congress Prints and Photographs Division.

TWO

THE SEDGWICKS OF STOCKBRIDGE

The Berkshires were renowned as a literary retreat by the mid-nineteenth century, when the poet Henry Wadsworth Longfellow traveled through the village of Stockbridge. On a visit to dine with Mrs. Sedgwick he enjoyed a twilight drive through the meadows and along the river. Later he wrote in his diary about spending a sociable evening at Samuel Ward's, listening to classical music.[1] "Mrs. [Fanny Kemble] Butler sang a ballad. —said that everything seemed to be Sedgwick in this region; the very grasshoppers in the field chirp, 'Sedgwick! Sedgwick!'"[2]

As Longfellow suggests, the Sedgwicks were a driving force behind the community. Two generations of the family had helped to shape Stockbridge—both through leadership in local and national politics and through genius in the oratory and literary arts. The Sedgwicks set high cultural and ideological standards that drew like-minded Americans and foreign visitors to this unique place in western Massachusetts, known for its idyllic landscape. In doing so, they helped to instill pride in the natural environment, respect for the village, and a sense of community, laying the groundwork for the nation's first village improvement society.

The year of the Mohicans' departure to upstate New York, Theodore Sedgwick moved his law practice from the village of Sheffield to Stockbridge, about fifteen miles northeast. A New York senator, Sedgwick was well known throughout the region, most recently for winning one of the first civil rights cases involving slavery. In 1780 an enslaved woman known as Bett had appeared at his Sheffield office and requested his help in granting her freedom. Bett was a slave in the home of Col. John Ashley, a judge in the Berkshire Court of Common Pleas who was one of a group, including Sedgwick, responsible for drafting the Sheffield Declaration. This landmark 1773 statute granted freedom to "mankind" three years before the Declaration of Independence, and both led to a revision in the Massachusetts constitution, which further clarified individual freedom in 1780.

When Bett approached Sedgwick, she understood that her rights were now openly defined in political terms. Her eloquent appeal for personal liberty challenged the lawyer to test the validity of the new constitution. Sedgwick enlisted Tapping Reeve, founder of the Litchfield Law School, and another of Ashley's slaves, Brom, to bolster the case. In 1781 the jury ruled in Bett's favor, making her the first Black woman to be set free under the Massachusetts state constitution. Later that year her case was cited as precedent in the successful freedom suit of Quock Walker, which ended the practice of slavery in the state. Upon receiving her freedom, Bett changed her name to Elizabeth Freeman and accepted a position as a paid servant in the Sedgwick household.[3]

In the late eighteenth century, residents began to see significant signs of cultural progress throughout the Berkshires. Four elms were planted on Main Street by a grandson of Jonathan Edwards to celebrate the signing of the nation's Constitution.[4] The first paper in the region, the Stockbridge *Western Star,* was printed

Yale-Duryea Mills, East Main Street, Stockbridge, 1934. Library of Congress Prints and Photographs Division.

by Loring Andrews beginning in 1789. A year later, twenty-five residents had chartered the Stockbridge Library Society.[5] None of these achievements were remarkable—New Haven had its stately elms in 1686, social libraries dated back to the 1760s in more populous parts of Massachusetts, and the *Hartford Courant* had been printing the news since 1764—but to the white settlers who grew up in "Indian Town," civilization seemed to have conquered the wilderness. When a commission appointed by Congress finally established the boundary between Massachusetts and New York, the borders of their community felt secure.[6]

The village of Stockbridge offered fledgling cultural amenities but little in the way of industry. Elijah Williams's enterprises continued to flourish in West Stockbridge, where a single dam on the Williams River supplied a gristmill, stone mill, and sawmill before the turn of the century. "Old Quarry," on the west bank of the river, had become profitable by 1790, and soon entrepreneurs were investing in mining local marble.[7] Known for its "quality and beauty," the marble was sought after from "all parts of the country, East, South and West," eventually furnishing the material for such major buildings as New York City Hall (1811).[8] In nearby Curtisville and Glendale, as well as West Stockbridge, factories produced paper, textiles, furniture, and leather goods. Local sawmills and lumber yards were now beginning to distribute their goods regionally.

•

In the winter of 1789, just a few days before the new year, the Sedgwick family welcomed Catharine Maria, their sixth child. Her mother struggled with mental illness and her father traveled frequently, leaving her in the care of two much older sisters. Despite this inauspicious beginning, Catharine would grow up to become an author esteemed in educated circles throughout the nation and abroad. Her early writings attest to her deep love and respect for her surrogate mother, Elizabeth Freeman (fondly known as Mumbet), a person she not only admired but strove to emulate. Although Catharine formed equally strong bonds with her brothers, Freeman instilled in her a fundamental sense of security essential to her future success.

When Catharine was a young adult, Freeman purchased a house on Cherry Hill, outside of the town proper. By 1790 eleven Black families lived in the area extending from the "Negro Swamp" (now Lake Agawam) at the base of Monument Mountain to Cherry Hill Road.[9] In 1807, Freeman added a twelve-acre parcel around "Negro Pond" to her legacy. Catharine took notice of Freeman's achievements, both material and spiritual. As an older woman, she wrote that the more she knew and observed of "human nature, the higher does she [Freeman] rise above others, whatever may have been their instruction or accomplishment."[10] Like Freeman, Sedgwick shared Aupaumut's belief in the ability to see

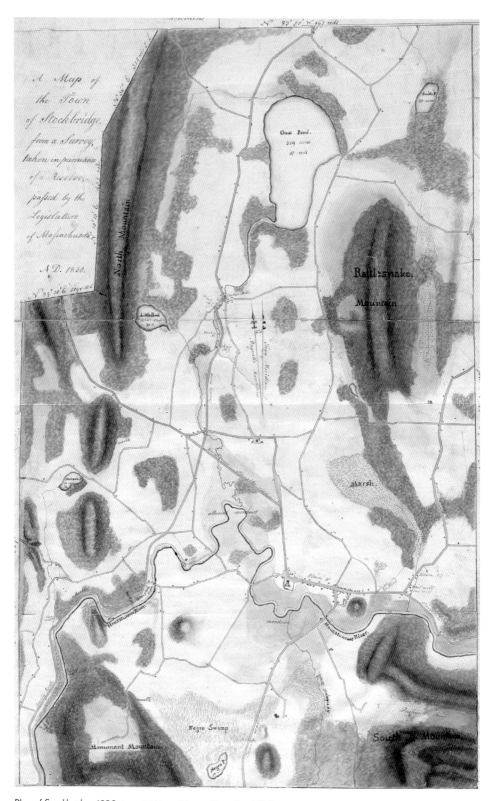

Plan of Stockbridge, 1830. Leventhal Map & Education Center Digital Collections.

humanity across all races and to value human dignity above all, essential qualities that would differentiate her literary work from the didactic prose of the day.

The Sedgwicks were part of an elite circle in Stockbridge, but their association with New York City placed them in an upper echelon of American society. At a time when university degrees were rare, Theodore Sedgwick Jr. followed in the footsteps of his father, graduating from Yale in 1798. The younger Sedgwick sons would most likely have reinforced this tradition were it not for the establishment of Williams College, about thirty-five miles to the north. This new institution, founded in 1793, educated Henry and Robert. Their mother, Pamela, traced her lineage to the founding of Stockbridge, and her relatives included Ephraim Williams Jr., the original patron of the college. Theodore continued to ascend the political ladder, becoming a state supreme court justice in 1802.

As a member of this cultured family, Catharine was encouraged to read widely and to appreciate the beauty of her surroundings. She sometimes traveled with her father, "an observer and lover of nature," sharing conversations about politics and world affairs. In the evenings the family would stay up until nine listening to his readings of Hume, Shakespeare, *Don Quixote,* and *Hudibras,* Samuel Butler's popular satirical poem. These great works of literature swept her away to realms of thought and feeling far from the closely monitored world of the Stockbridge elite. She developed the habit of thinking for herself. Her rich home life, both in Stockbridge and in New York, provided a more valuable education than that typically offered a young woman of her era.[11]

For Catharine Sedgwick, the death of her father in 1813 was both painful and affirming. Theodore was stricken with a life-threatening illness during a family trip to Boston. As he lay dying, he confessed to doubting his religious faith but feeling powerless to reject the ministrations of his friend the Congregational minister Stephen West. On his deathbed, he converted to Unitarianism, most likely with the help of Catharine, who had contacted William Ellery Channing. The famous Unitarian minister provided the necessary solace to Theodore and also awakened Catharine's own latent religious doubts.[12]

The division of religious faith in the Sedgwick family reflected the great changes occurring throughout New England during the early national period, a time when Puritan religious principles began to be superseded by Unitarianism and religious revivals. As the Industrial Revolution gained momentum, even the small village of Stockbridge saw the impact of steam power, which expanded the production capacity of new cylinder and rotary printing presses. Printing advancements made books and periodicals affordable and led to the development of new institutions for cultural improvement, a growing emphasis on domestication, a widespread belief in the value of gentility, and an attraction to ornament, craft, and design as evidence of good taste.[13]

By the early nineteenth century the Berkshires had begun to draw residents seeking culture as well as beauty. In 1807, Elkanah Watson, founder of the state bank of Albany, retreated from state politics to a more bucolic setting, where he began to put into practice his ideas for promoting civic improvement. Watson purchased a 250-acre farm a mile from Pittsfield and, as one of his first attempts to improve rural life, exhibited two Merino sheep at the great elm tree in the town's public square. His effort to inspire animal husbandry was the first such display of farm animals in the nation. It was also the catalyst for the country's first organized agricultural fair in October 1811. The following year Watson became the founding president of the Berkshire Agricultural Society. In addition to promoting "modern" farming methods, the organization offered premiums to citizens for the best submissions of animals and agricultural products. Annual exhibitions, or "farmers' holidays," included elaborate processions of oxen, stages displaying examples of American manufactures, and parades of members.[14]

Two years after the society's founding, Watson hoped to enrich his organization by giving "the excited minds" of women "a direction which will promote their happiness and independence," and also boost the national economy. He encouraged women to participate by offering premiums for domestic manufactures, holding an agricultural ball, and including the reading of pastoral odes at meetings. A visionary, Watson seemed oblivious to the conventions limiting the roles of women in public affairs. He was surprised when female premium winners refused to enter the society building to pick up their prizes, but solved the problem by having his wife superintend the awards.[15] Watson's ultimate goal was to guarantee an "independent America, free of debt to the Old World," by developing American agriculture and domestic manufactures.[16]

One of the featured participants in the 1818 Berkshire Agricultural Fair was a young poet named William Cullen Bryant. Three years earlier, Bryant had moved from rural Cummington, about forty-five miles east, to Great Barrington in the hope of furthering himself as an attorney. He soon met Charles Sedgwick and became a member of the Berkshire bar. In the meantime, Bryant's father had instigated the publication of his son's poem "Thanatopsis," an ode to "love of nature" that attracted the attention of literary circles in New York and Boston. The title translated as "A Consideration of Death," but the poem was more a meditation on the spirit of the surrounding wilderness—the uplifting nature of New England—than a reflection on that serious topic. Publication brought him notice, and Bryant began to accept invitations to speak at local events, including a gathering of the Great Barrington Bible Society, where he delivered a treatise cleverly disguising his Unitarian beliefs.

When he wrote the town's Fourth of July speech in 1820, Bryant was known for his literary talent, though hardly appreciated as a harbinger of national literary prowess. That year, Charles Sedgwick introduced him to his sister Catharine, who was also considered literary but not yet a published author. The two developed an intense, supportive friendship, and, along with her brothers, Catharine encouraged Bryant to further his career, resulting in his move to New York City in the mid-1820s.[17] Before leaving, Bryant wrote his most famous Berkshire poem, "Monument Mountain," a tribute to the regional landscape of the Mohicans. His poem tells the story of an Indian maiden, tormented by love for her cousin, who leaps from a precipice rather than betray tribal rules against intermarriage. To honor her spirit, members of the tribe "Built up a simple monument, a cone / Of small loose stones" over her grave. Bryant's poem was an effort to explain the existence of this monument and why "Indians from the distant West, who come / To visit where their fathers' bones are laid, / Yet tell this sorrowful tale." Soon the "Mountain of the Monument" became a pilgrimage site for locals and tourists as well.

•

Born just a few years after the Mohicans left Stockbridge, Catharine grew up in a town permeated with the memory of their culture, a heritage she and her fellow New Englanders were beginning to mythologize as part of America's founding story. Her first manuscript began as a religious tract exposing the evils of "Calvinistic Protestantism," intended as a gift to her new church.[18] She was working on it during the summer of 1821, when she traveled to upstate New York hoping to visit a "far away" cousin. Writing from Niagara Falls, she told her relatives not to be surprised that "Indian blood is mingled in his veins."[19] When she returned home and showed her brother Harry the completed tract, he suggested she recast her observations as fiction. The story incorporated the landscape surrounding her home—its hills, crags, rivers, and native flora and fauna. Within this natural context, she commented on the American character and religion, relinquishing a Puritan/Calvinist past for the "new" Unitarian ideology. *A New-England Tale; Or Sketches of New-England Character and Manners,* published in 1822, sold out in less than two months.[20]

As the Berkshires became thickly settled, transportation improved and residents could depend on a daily coach making trips between Albany and Boston.[21] The pace of life increased for wealthy families like the Sedgwicks who spent part of the year in New York City. In 1824, Bryant met James Fenimore Cooper at their New York residence, a literary salon of sorts. Back in Stockbridge, a new Congregational church was built on a "site less bleak and more convenient"— the green at the west end of the village, near the location of the original mission church.[22] Theodore Sedgwick Jr., now president of the Berkshire Agricultural Society, initiated discussions with regional leaders about introducing a railroad to the area, and in 1826 wrote a series of newspaper articles on the subject, the first effort to establish county train lines.

By the second decade of the century, educational opportunities had improved for women with means, and five residents of Stockbridge were graduates of Sarah Pierce's Female Academy in Litchfield, Connecticut.[23] Archibald Hopkins sent his niece Huldah Hopkins there in 1817, a particularly generous gesture as he was her guardian.[24] Huldah's sister, Lucinda, was tutored by her cousin, Catharine Sedgwick, during the summer and spring of 1821.[25] Five years later, Lucinda and Mary Hopkins enrolled in Miss Pierce's school along with Emilia Field. By then, students were instructed in natural and moral philosophy, logic, chemistry, mathematics, and the Latin and Greek languages, as well as the "ornamental arts."[26] The academy owned a herbarium, a collection of dried flowers and ornamental plants that had been developed with some faculty from Williams College.[27] The sisters lived and learned with some of the Northeast's most educated and esteemed families—the daughters of ministers, politicians, and physicians. The experience was transformational for Mary Hopkins, who was only thirteen.[28]

When the Hopkins girls were away at school, Catharine Sedgwick published *Hope Leslie; or Early Times in the Massachusetts* (1827). For residents of Stock-

Catherine M. Sedgwick, c. 1832. Library of Congress Prints and Photographs Division.

bridge, the novel was close to home. The most dramatic scene in her historical romance occurs on a laurel-covered hill overlooking the Housatonic. Set in the seventeenth century, the story involves a loving childhood relationship between the daughter of a Pequot chief and the son of a prominent colonist, as well as a congenial interracial marriage. Sedgwick reconstructed portions of the 1704 Deerfield Massacre while also drawing on an event that had recently caused a considerable stir in Cornwall, Connecticut—the marriage of her cousin Harriet Gold to Elias Boudinot, a Cherokee.[29] If aspects of her narrative seem contrived today, Sedgwick's deep understanding of how human relationships transcend race seemed plausible to fellow readers, many of whom also shared "Indian blood." *Hope Leslie* was an instant best seller, rivaling the success of the *Leatherstocking Tales* and bringing a new wave of attention to its author.

After the release of *Hope Leslie,* Catharine moved to Lenox and joined the household of her brother Charles, a town clerk since 1821, his wife, Elizabeth Dwight Sedgwick, and their children. Her move coincided with Elizabeth's decision to open a school for girls. Already considered a woman of "wide and distinguished acquaintance," Elizabeth became known for educating successful girls of accomplished families. Among her students were Ellen Emerson, daughter of Ralph Waldo, the sculptor Harriet Hosmer, author Maria Susanna Cummins, and the daughters of Wayman Crow, a St. Louis businessman and cofounder of Washington University. Catharine played a role in the school, adding luster to Lenox at a time when her work was garnering international acclaim.[30]

•

Sedgwick's novels celebrated the unique American landscape as citizens were learning about a new movement to improve civic space through tree planting. Stockbridge residents knew of the four elms growing by the post office, but these were commemorative trees.[31] As early as 1828, Thomas Green Fessenden, editor of the *New England Farmer,* advocated for widespread tree planting for sheer public enjoyment. Through articles in his popular magazine published out of Boston, Fessenden laid the groundwork for the tree-planting initiatives Andrew Jackson Downing espoused decades later. Fessenden also argued for executing improvement plans that would lead to "an increase in solid wealth and comfort," such as the installation of sidewalks.[32] In 1830, perhaps thanks to Fessenden's lobbying, the Massachusetts General Court passed a statute protecting ornamental and shade trees growing along streets and highways. A fine of five dollars (more than $150 today) was leveled for deliberately damaging a roadside tree on public land. The Concord Ornamental Tree Society, the earliest known tree-planting group in America, had formed by 1834, and "began by ornamenting the public squares and grounds in the centre of the town, with the view of extending their operations in every direction." Mention of the Concord society's founding appeared in local newspapers, the *New England Farmer,* and J. C. Loudon's *Gardener's Magazine,* based in London.[33]

During these early years of the tree-planting movement, Theodore Sedgwick Jr. led the Berkshire County Agricultural Society's efforts to build state support for the county's economic diversification. Subsistence farming had become less viable, and he felt strongly that for Massachusetts to retain its population, those in power must sponsor social and public projects encouraging new agricultural industries.[34] Sedgwick circulated new theories about the relationship between social reform and landscape improvement which were picked up in popular journals. Andrew Jackson Downing had just begun his career as a scientific horticulturist and landscape gardener, developing his ideas in articles for the *Magazine of Horticulture, Horticultural Register, New-York Farmer,* and *New England Farmer.*[35]

Mary Hopkins was most likely exposed to the literature of progressive farming through her uncle Archibald. She also learned about landscape gardening and design related to the work of his sons, Mark and Albert, who would both go on to distinguished careers at Williams College. In 1833, Albert, a professor of mathematics, natural philosophy, and astronomy, organized a landscape gardening society at the school and launched natural history expeditions. Having admired educational institutions and parks on his trips to Europe, he had trees planted and graded walks built on the campus and galvanized his students to create a public park in Williamstown. Mark Hopkins joined the Williams faculty in 1830 and became president of the college just three years later. Both believed landscape improvements influenced "great moral improvement among the young men."[36]

Testaments to the value of improving the American landscape and its villages also appeared in fiction of the day. In "Pedlar Karl," a story published in the London *New Monthly Magazine,* the popular writer N. P. Willis makes a point of mentioning his experience of English landscapes before introducing the "fairest village" he had ever seen. Unlike most American small towns, characterized by "traces of *newness,*" Stockbridge was "an old town," with swards of grass, picturesque bridges, and majestic elms—a village "embowered in foliage." For Willis, however, the "greatest attraction of all [was] the authoress of 'Redwood' and 'Hope Leslie,' a novelist of whom America has the good sense to be proud, . . . the Miss Mitford of Stockbridge." Without mentioning Sedgwick by name, Willis observed that women could serve as effective instigators for improving village life. "A *man,* though a distinguished one, may have little influence on the town he lives in; but a remarkable *woman* is the invariable cynosure of a community, and irradiates it all. . . . 'Our Village' [Stockbridge] does not look like other villages."[37]

"Main Street, looking East, Stockbridge," 1912. Postcard.

After the publication of *Hope Leslie*, Laurel Hill became a place of pilgrimage for Sedgwick's readers, who recognized the landmark from her rich description in the novel. Like the protagonists in her story, visitors "entered the expanded vale, by following the windings of the Housatonick around a hill, conical and easy of ascent, excepting on that side which overlooked the river. . . . On every other side, the hill was garlanded with laurels, now in full and profuse bloom; here and there surmounted by an intervening pine, spruce, or hemlock, whose seared winter foliage was fringed with the bright tender sprouts of spring."[38] When Laurel Hill was threatened by the craze for industrial mining, Sedgwick took it on herself to protect the landscape.[39] She had already urged a Dr. Pomeroy not to support the "establishment of a Home for Discharged Convicts," which she saw as an affront to the beauty of the village as well as its moral health.[40] In 1834 the Sedgwick family purchased Laurel Hill from J. A. Woodbridge and put it under the care of trustees as a community "pleasure ground." A romantic location with a legendary past, Laurel Hill was now a destination offering visitors a sense of the "New World's" natural beauty. The first public gathering at the hill occurred that summer in honor of the Marquis de Lafayette's death.[41]

Among those who sought Sedgwick's acquaintance in Stockbridge during this time were three of the most famous women of letters in Britain: the renowned actress and author Fanny Kemble, the political economist Harriet Martineau, and the celebrated art historian Anna Brownell Jameson. The presence of such intellectual figures marked the beginning of the region's development into an American "Lake District," a retreat especially popular among writers.[42] Stockbridge residents could now receive a letter just thirteen hours after it left New York, a marvel Sedgwick described to her brother Robert as an "annihilation of space which our forefathers never dreamed."[43] Within a few years, passenger rail service was established from West Stockbridge to Hudson, New York, where trains crossed the Hudson River on the way into the city. Public transportation to Boston was still only by stagecoach.

Catharine Sedgwick's appreciation of Stockbridge, and the Berkshire landscape as a whole, was best expressed in letters written during a visit to Europe in 1839 and later compiled into a book. Throughout her journey she made observations of value to her "kindred at home," asking them to imagine a "hill rising from the bosom of meadows as our Laurel Hill does, but twice as high and twice as steep," comparing Baden, the celebrated German watering place, to "the northern towns in our own Berkshire," and recalling "drives through the Connecticut River meadows" while vising the ruins of Godesberg Castle. She ridiculed the English for assuming that American society existed only in New York City (exclaiming, "Oh, genii locorum of our little inland villages, forgive them!"), but admired the continent's public parks. She wrote of America's "folly" in leaving "such narrow spaces for what has been so well called the lungs of a city" and wondered whether "anything [had] been done to secure the refinement of pleasure-grounds in our smaller towns and villages." If lacking the means to rival English parks, her countrywomen "with taste and industry" might bring the plants of the forest to their homes.[44] Sedgwick felt justifiably proud of her family's effort to preserve a healthy breathing spot in her native village.

Although her observations were unique, Sedgwick's thoughts about the importance of parks and tasteful, well-maintained villages were part of a national conversation among the elite eager to improve American architecture and landscape. *Letters from Abroad to Kindred at Home* seemed to have had an immediate effect. In 1841, the year of its publication, residents voluntarily cleared brush and leaves from Laurel Hill.[45] Sedgwick's call for improving the village landscape would continue to play a role in Stockbridge's growing conception of itself as an ideal New England town as well as a destination worthy of foreign visitors eager to experience authentic early American village life.

The notable interest in natural features, especially those close to home, was publicly displayed at the Berkshire Jubilee, a two-day county celebration in Pittsfield. During the summer of 1844, the region's most accomplished citizens gathered to praise rural and civic achievements. "The Stockbridge Bowl" by the local poet Lydia Sigourney paid tribute to "the beautiful sheet of water, forming a pond, in the north part of the town."[46] Sigourney's poem is also an ode to an idyllic past, as she describes "the Indian hunter," Magawisca (Sedgwick's Pequot heroine), wild animals, famous statesmen, and humble students—all returning to the beautiful Berkshire Hills.[47] Another orator called on the audience to listen to the teachings of Pittsfield's revered elm, a 126-foot-tall, 250-year-old tree that had witnessed surprising improvements "in hills, vallies, [and] limped streams," the former "greatly beautified by the hand of man," and the latter "pressed into his service."[48] The Jubilee was a celebration of heritage and nature as well as a means for building upon both.

Stockbridge Bowl from Shadow Brook, 1900–1920. Library of Congress Prints and Photographs Division.

The desire to preserve and improve America's landscape manifested at the Jubilee was also being expressed through national discussions of park design. A month before the event, William Cullen Bryant wrote an editorial in the *New York Evening Post* advocating for a public park in New York City.[49] Bryant's effort would eventually gain support from his friend the Reverend Orville Dewey, of nearby Sheffield, and Andrew Jackson Downing. Downing's popular *Treatise on the Theory and Practice of Landscape Gardening,* revised and reissued in 1844, was unique in championing the rural cemetery as a public park that could enhance community life. Adept at communicating to a broad readership, Downing added the development of a central park for New York to his mission of improving the civic landscape.[50]

As editor of the *Horticulturalist,* the magazine he founded in 1846, Downing was the national tastemaker when it came to garden design and the importance of trees as ornaments of homes and towns. New England villages, he declared, were "as beautiful as any in the world," owing to their "sylvan charms," a quality dependent, in large part, on shade trees.[51] He advised leaders of rural towns (such as the Laurel Hill Association) to plant indigenous trees, which were more likely not only to survive but also to reach perfection as a species and therefore impart further beauty to local streets. Stockbridge was singled out for its sugar maples, "the rural glory of the place."[52]

In the autumn of 1849, when he was at the height of his fame, Downing invited Catharine Sedgwick to Highland Gardens, his home and nursery in Newburgh, New York. The occasion was a visit from the internationally renowned Swedish author Fredrika Bremer, who had embarked on a two-year trip across America in search of material for her next book. The author of *Morning Watches, Life in Sweden,* and *The Neighbors,* among other novels of everyday life, Bremer was known for her ability to depict emotions and natural settings realistically. Having corresponded with Bremer for several years, Downing was honored to host the celebrity author and chose Sedgwick, whom he considered her American counterpart, as a cultured addition to their party.

A highlight of the visit was a trek up South Beacon Mountain, with its awe-inspiring view of the Hudson River, a picturesque American landscape all admired. The three traveled in a carriage together and enjoyed an outdoor meal of capon and champagne. At the time, the visit was a casual, country holiday among like-minded peers. In retrospect, the event illustrated the new republic's progress in building national aesthetics, its achievements in transportation, and the affinity between the growing writers' retreat in the Berkshires and the Hudson River School of painters, who were enmeshed in New York City culture. Sedgwick wrote a letter to her niece recounting her meeting with the famous Swedish novelist, who later visited her in Lenox. After leav-

View from Beacon Mountain, 1905. Postcard.

ing Highland Gardens, Bremer documented her journey through America in long letters to Downing and his wife. The publication of *The Homes of the New World; Impressions of America* (1853), which included her story of meeting Downing and Sedgwick, would bring her discoveries to an international readership.[53]

Bremer's journey illustrated the ease with which those of means could travel, from the Astor Hotel in New York to the Hudson River Valley, by railroad, steamer, and carriage. The Stockbridge & Pittsfield Railroad line was completed in 1849, finally providing the village with direct passenger rail service to New York City and Boston. Business trips soon expanded into summer sojourns with family members in tow, mostly traveling from New York and Boston.[54] The railroad had a profound and unexpected effect on the region's economy. Local industries struggled to compete with the influx of goods coming in by rail, an issue that stifled new efforts at production. At the same time, the rail connection brought in tourists, usually affluent and planning to stay for more than a few days. Those in search of natural beauty were particularly eager to visit Stockbridge, the most scenic of the villages. The region came to be known for its landscape—the serene Housatonic River, rolling hills, and expansive meadows.[55]

A legendary hike up Monument Mountain hosted by David Dudley Field on August 5, 1850, further enhanced the reputation of the Berkshires as a scenic literary retreat and remains one of the region's most beloved historical narratives. Three guests took the train to Stockbridge from Pittsfield: Oliver Wendell Holmes, who had built a summer home there the year before; Herman Melville; and the publisher Evert Duyckinck. They were joined by Field, Nathaniel Hawthorne, who was in the midst of completing his manuscript of *The House*

View from Monument Mountain, c. 1850–1920. Digital Commonwealth.

of the Seven Gables, and others eager to summit the famous peak. The festivities included champagne and a reading of William Cullen Bryant's poem honoring the revered mountain. Although a thunderstorm broke up the party, the bad weather played a fortuitous role in American literary history: when Hawthorne and Melville sought shelter from the storm, they struck up a friendship that would prove crucial to the younger author's completion of his current novel, *Moby-Dick.* The experience also led Melville to buy property adjacent Holmes's residence, a 1780 farmhouse he named Arrowhead.[56]

The literary prestige of Stockbridge at midcentury was well documented in *Homes of American Authors,* a collection of essays on seventeen prominent writers and their home grounds. Hawthorne, Bryant, and Longfellow were among those profiled. In this elite company, Sedgwick stood out as the only woman and arguably the author most associated with her hometown and its surroundings. Stockbridge had realized "the beau-ideal of a village," its "neat dwellings, indic-

"The Sedgwick Mansion, Birthplace of C. M. Sedgwick." From *Homes of American Authors.*

ative of cultivated and refined proprietors, an aspect rather idiosyncratic in our land." The village displayed "no architectural absurdity," but showed rather "a reverence for the past, demonstrated in a careful repair and scrupulous preservation of ancestral homes." Several houses were owned by women, a fact the author considered a sound argument for women's rights. To illustrate the landscape of surrounding wilderness tamed by design, *Homes* included a description of an old man walking the "well-trodden paths" winding around Laurel Hill, the setting Sedgwick had made famous.[57]

Indian Monument, Stockbridge, c. 1900–1920. Library of Congress Prints and Photographs Division.

THREE

THE LAUREL HILL ASSOCIATION

By 1852, when Electa Jones was finishing her book, the literary elite had secured Stockbridge's reputation as a prosperous village, esteemed for its natural beauty. Jones, however, was more interested in recording the periodicals picked up at the South Post Office, clearly an "index of the taste and principles of the people." These numbered more than sixty titles ranging from the *Sailor's Magazine* to the *Boston Culturist, Phrenological Journal,* and *London Quarterly Review.*[1] Her local history briefly mentions various charitable and community efforts over the years—including societies devoted to enhancing shrubbery, keeping the church in good repair, and maintaining the South graveyard—but these were short-lived efforts focused on small civic improvements.

The newly established Elm Tree Association, founded by Orville Dewey, had higher aspirations for the town of Sheffield. The group's mission was to enhance the community landscape through tree planting, grading, sidewalk construction, and other projects intended to improve the "human condition." Members met annually under the famous Sheffield Elm, where speeches were made, followed by refreshments.[2] Although not designated a village improvement organization, the Elm Tree Association appears to have functioned as such during its short existence.[3] According to the local author Walter Prichard Eaton, Mary Hopkins attended the association's spring 1853 meeting and was voted an honorary member.[4] This experience may have been the catalyst for her founding of the Laurel Hill Association.

Despite its reputation as one of the most beautiful villages of the Berkshires, by midcentury Stockbridge appears to have been in need of improvement. Main Street was poorly graded, pocked with pools of water in the spring and lined by

"Old elm, Sheffield, Mass." New York Public Library Digital Collections.

gullies filled with garbage; walks were few and rarely repaired. The cemetery, partially enclosed by a battered wooden fence, offered little in the way of shade or seating for those who wished to linger. The beauty of Stockbridge had been marred by public use and lack of maintenance.[5] Twentieth-century accounts of Mary Hopkins's motivation for founding the LHA describe her outrage at recognizing the degradation of her hometown. One popular history has her astride a white horse riding "up hill, down dale," seeking to educate the "unprogressive" and even "swooping down from the saddle to whisk up a bit of waste paper."[6] In another version of the LHA's origin story, passed down over the years, Hopkins is visiting the graves of Grandmother Electa Sergeant and Great-Grandfather John Sergeant. The broken cemetery fence allows cows to wander freely and graze on the grass among the bramble-covered graves. Trees are scarce. An affront to both the living and the dead, the cemetery hardly reflects the refinement of Stockbridge's citizens.[7] Surveying the scene from horseback, she resolves to take action.

The charismatic leader portrayed in these accounts is not found in the early records of the association or in contemporary newspaper coverage. Once she launched the organization in the summer of 1853, Hopkins stayed in the background. The founding of a volunteer civic association was no small task, particularly if projects involved community property. Her confidence may have been boosted by knowledge of a new state law, passed that May, which allowed groups of ten or more individuals who "by agreement in writing, associate for the purpose of encouraging agriculture, horticulture, or improving and ornamenting the streets and public squares of any city or town, by planting and cultivating ornamental trees therein" to incorporate, like social libraries and lyceums, and granting them "all the like rights, powers and privileges as the proprietors of such libraries."[8] News of this statute came from Rep. John Zacheus Goodrich, who had recently been elected to Congress and served as Stockbridge justice of the peace. A native of Sheffield, his friends and family were members of the Elm Tree Association.

When Hopkins began planning the initial meeting of her civic-minded society, she likely consulted Goodrich for advice. In addition to assuring the group's legal status, the former newspaperman was an officer of the Stockbridge & Pittsfield Railroad Company and eager to offer his assistance in an initiative dedicated to economic improvement.[9] Goodrich's friend Charles M. Owen, also on the railroad board, presided over the Housatonic Bank, the only such financial institution in Stockbridge. Owen's status as vice president of the Berkshire Horticultural Society assured his support for the association's efforts in taking out loans and building an endowment.

Mary Hopkins Goodrich, n.d. Courtesy
Stockbridge Library Museum & Archives.

Mary Hopkins understood the essential role that strong community connections would play in achieving village improvement. Her list of speakers for the inaugural meeting included prominent relatives: her cousin Mark Hopkins, brothers-in-law David Dudley and Jonathan Field, and distant cousins Charles and Theodore Sedgwick. In addition to Goodrich and Owen, she invited another brother-in-law, Rev. Henry M. Field, an international scholar on evangelical work.[10] She was also encouraged by the successful efforts of the "Women of Stockbridge," "noble and patriotic ladies" who had recently organized a fair to raise money to support the former Hungarian president Lajos Kossuth's campaign for freedom in Hungary.[11]

On August 22, 1853, townspeople discovered notices posted in prominent public gathering places throughout Stockbridge. A few passed by, uninterested

Old Bank Building, Stockbridge. Library of Congress Prints and Photographs Division.

or illiterate or both, but those who could read learned about an upcoming town meeting. All residents were invited "to take measures for the regular improvement of the Burying Ground, the streets, the walks, the public grounds and Laurel Hill." Two days later, the curious gathered on the hill, where some of the most respected citizens endorsed a new effort to improve the village. A group of powerful orators elicited "much enthusiasm" from the crowd. The event ended by generating a "warrant" formally identifying the citizens "associated for the purpose of improving and ornamenting the streets and public squares of the Town of Stockbridge, by planting and cultivating ornamental trees therein." In addition to Hopkins, six other women were mentioned as "associates," including her sister Huldah F. Field. A copy of the warrant was posted at the "Post-Office of the Plain," announcing the inaugural meeting at the Old Academy.[12]

When Goodrich called the meeting to order on September 3, the assembled group voted to preserve Laurel Hill "for the benefit and pleasure of the public" and became the first to take full advantage of the new state legislation authorizing the improvement of cities and towns. From its founding, the Laurel Hill Association followed the rules of incorporation and, bolstered by this legal status, not only sustained itself but embellished its mission. After adopting by-laws, officers and the twelve members of the executive committee were selected, with Charles Owen chosen as president pro tem. The four vice presidents—a judge, the Congregational minister, the Episcopalian minister, and a physician—comprised a broad representation of prominent citizens. The clerk, E. W. B. Canning, would prove one of the most devoted members, serving for more than three decades and regularly contributing poems celebrating the region's cultural landscape. Although the only female officer was a corresponding secretary, eight women served on the executive committee. Honorary members included David D. Field, Theodore and Charles Sedgwick, and Mark and Albert Hopkins. From its founding, the association welcomed as members all residents who committed themselves to "planting and protecting a tree under the Executive Committee." Those who preferred not to plant paid a membership fee of one dollar over three years. Children under fourteen were given the same tree-planting opportunity or paid twenty-five cents for membership.[13]

On September 19, the association convened to launch its business before winter set in. Although little could be accomplished before the following spring, the association had organized itself into five standing committees, each responsible for a discrete section of the village. An officer was placed at the helm of each committee, guaranteeing that leaders were committed to managing and executing specific projects. From the beginning, the association focused on improving the entire village center and guaranteeing its future maintenance. The LHA's well-planned projects and carefully considered allocation of resources established a solid foundation for moving forward. Clerk Canning would later recall that "the natural beauty of Stockbridge is conspicuous; but during the year 1853, Miss Mary G. Hopkins . . . conceived the plan of enhancing the gifts of Nature by the hands of Art, and of uniting every age, sex, and occupation in the undertaking."[14]

When work resumed in the spring, the LHA continued to improve the cemetery. For expertise on hardy hedges, the burying ground committee consulted Downing's *Rural Essays,* a collection of his writings from the *Horticulturist* with an introductory "letter" (actually a posthumous tribute) by Fredrika Bremer. Downing greatly esteemed the Norway spruce, "perhaps the most popular foreign evergreen" and one he considered particularly suited to the northern states, "where an unfailing shelter, screen, and barrier, are wanted at *all seasons.*" At a time when buckthorn and Osage orange were all the rage for deciduous hedges, the committee demonstrated its confidence in Downing by choosing a tree that he predicted would become the most popular for evergreen hedges. The executive committee appropriated one hundred dollars to this "experiment."[15]

By this time the association had created a sophisticated plan for improving the village infrastructure. At meetings the five committees were held accountable for their work and encouraged to discuss challenges and potential solutions with the group. In June and July, much was accomplished. Committee no. 2 improved the grounds of the Congregational church and placed a railing near an adjacent house to prevent horse carriages from driving on the church green. Committee no. 3 attended to the "area from Mrs. Dwight's corner around the Academy to Hon. J. Z. Goodrich's house." Members of committee no. 4, responsible for the "park by [the] hotel, grounds in front of Episcopal Church and up the hill," were laying the stone causeway over Main Street and had removed the railing around the park, trimmed trees, and cleared brush. Committee no. 5, dedicated to improving the cemetery, benefited from a $200 contribution from E. Watson Pomeroy of Missouri obtained through Mary Hopkins. Special subcommittees appointed on an ad hoc basis carried out specific improvement projects such as regrading a road, building a watercourse, or planning a new sidewalk.[16]

With its corporate structure in place and committee projects launched, the association devoted itself to tree planting, a cause that had long occupied the minds of New England villagers interested in improving their communities. Members planted 40 trees along Main Street and 229 in the cemetery, while villagers were encouraged to plant more than 150 additional trees in both locations. In early September 1854 the tree planting effort was supported by a contest with monetary prizes contributed by financier Cyrus West Field. The association committed itself to giving fifty cents to anyone who "set" a tree in a location designated by the committee within the grounds of the brick meetinghouse. Rules

View of the Cemetery, 1878. Courtesy Stockbridge Library Museum & Archives.

stipulated a deadline of July 1, 1855, and no payment was made unless the tree was "alive and thrifty" on August 1, 1856. Deciduous trees were to be at least ten feet tall and evergreens at least six feet. The association literally put a premium on tree planting by offering ten dollars to those who planted the fifteen best trees and the greatest number of hardy forest or fruit trees.[17]

In his lengthy Anniversary Day speech, former Stockbridge resident Stephen Burrall spoke of how trees "pay," not only by providing physical comforts through timber and shade, but also in terms of human happiness. Quoting from Downing's "Essay on Planting Shade Trees," he observed that "it is unluckily no one's especial business to ornament the streets," and applauded the association for taking charge of a task that had previously gone unattended. Burrall appreciated the need to clear trees as well, so that villagers might enjoy the view from a mountain summit and take in the "daily miracle" of sunrise.[18]

The election of Dr. Lucius S. Adams, the village physician, as its first official president included a formal announcement of the association's status as "a permanent affair." Now two years old, the group redefined its ambitions to include long-term goals with a comprehensive, even lofty, agenda. By shading sidewalks, eradicating "noxious" plant material, regulating drainage, and generally beautifying the village scene, members would garner their village regional recognition. To cast its desire for widespread admiration in a more godly light, the association aspired to "a Higher Purpose": Art and Nature would be united in perfect harmony, achieving perfection under its programming and care.[19]

"Perfected" was the word used to describe the association's vision of public ways in the village. Extensive attention went into defining, leveling, and designing the "high-way and sidewalks and water-courses," as well as creating new pedestrian paths, including a route to a footbridge to be built on South Street providing access to the railroad station. Among the projects listed were a sidewalk in front of the meetinghouse green with a sluice to divert water from the western rise of the village into the meadows and a similar watercourse east of the hotel. Views of the Housatonic were considered an essential attribute of the region's rural beauty, and keeping them open required vigilance. If these achievements seem commonplace today, at the time they were unprecedented efforts of a group of volunteers, who were also raising funds and planning, coordinating, and executing projects. In its devotion to enhancing Stockbridge's natural beauty, the

"South Street and Bridge, Stockbridge," n.d. Postcard.

association carried out initiatives that successive generations would delegate to landscape architects and planners.[20]

Trees were viewed as essential elements of the improvement work, and during the productive summer of 1855, the LHA planted four hundred Norway spruce as a hedge surrounding three sides of the cemetery. The next year, twenty spruce trees were planted on the meetinghouse green and an additional one hundred were set, seventy-five for an enlargement to the cemetery and twenty-five at the "Brick Church green." Having "wintered well," the cemetery hedge was now showing "a pleasing line of permanent green around its borders." The example set by the LHA was having an effect, and members noticed that citizens were now more conscientious in regard to their dooryards, flower gardens, and the general exterior appearance of their homes. Now members hoped the public interest in home improvement would extend beyond the village, "where there remains much to be done in side-walking and tree-planting."[21]

The first indication that the Laurel Hill Association's model for village improvement might reach a larger audience was seen that year when a "Rural Improvement Society" was established in Clinton, New York, the location of Hamilton College. E. W. B. Canning had brought news of the LHA to his friend Rev. B. W. Dwight, who spread the word to Hamilton faculty members. Because of its elite association with the college, however, the group would evolve into a "Rural Art Society," which diminished its effectiveness as a model for the typical New England village.[22]

Intent on continuing to perfect its vision, the LHA appointed two new committees in the fall of 1857, one charged with altering a walk on the south side of Main Street and the other with "consider[ing] the propriety of cutting out trees upon Laurel Hill so as to afford vistas upon the surrounding landscapes."[23] The stunning views from the hill would encompass a perfected New England village. These new initiatives reflected the association's efforts to define specific areas of town and to enhance Laurel Hill as a park and pleasure ground. Mary Hopkins served on the Laurel Hill committee, in addition to her regular work on furthering cemetery improvements. The year's annual report acknowledged her unflagging devotion to the village, pairing her with President Adams as the "effective force" of the organization.[24] Hopkins's influence would only increase after her marriage to John Z. Goodrich the next spring.

The first Anniversary Days were relatively unstructured festive gatherings, but beginning in 1858 the annual event honored town residents, Stockbridge's uniqueness, and the LHA's season of accomplishments.[25] The local holiday invented by the LHA institutionalized town consciousness and activism, increasing community spirit and securing a shared sense of the need to protect the character of the village. In following years, the event featured an annual formal banquet with a keynote speaker, often an individual of national renown. Typically held in late August, Anniversary Days were also public annual meetings attended by residents, summer sojourners, and other visitors, including many summering in nearby towns.

The *Berkshire County Eagle* recognized the importance of the association's Anniversary Day as "an occasion of interest to the whole county, . . . a Berkshire 'Institution,' designed for the adorning of Berkshire's historical town, as well as from the intrinsic merits of the mode of celebration."[26] In 1859 the event featured a keynote speech by William Ellery Sedgwick (which the *Eagle* later recommended printing as a pamphlet and circulating to the region's farmers) and a poem by S. B. Sumner of Great Barrington. The poet described the region's pastoral landscape—the "Old Housatonic" meandering through the meadows and the majestic elms—intertwining his description of natural history with recollections of the Stockbridge Indians, and observing all "clearly pictured today, in memory's rich panoramic display." The celebration continued into the evening, as more than two hundred participants joined the annual trek through "Icy Glen" by torchlight, a "wild procession" illuminating a "most strange and weird" landscape. A few days later, the *Eagle* announced that the event had created a stir throughout neighboring villages, along with news of "branches of the 'Laurel' taking root in various places."[27]

Within the next decade, the association oversaw three major building projects that clearly demonstrated its municipal power: the installation of running water to all buildings in the center of town, the construction of a library, and the mounting of gas streetlamps along Main Street. At a time when most villages in the United States were quagmires of filth and unsanitary practices, fresh water, access to books, and lighted streets were luxuries. Even more unusual, these amenities came through the hard work of volunteers whose only reward was pride in their community achievement.

The LHA largely succeeded in such extensive and costly ventures by securing large donations of both money and materials from members and their friends. Judge J. E. Field rallied seventeen subscribers to fund the town's first water company in 1862. He hired a civil engineer and a builder from Pittsfield to install more than forty pipes to carry fresh water from Beartown Mountain, at the cost of $9,000 (nearly $275,000 today). John Hamilton Gourlie, a former president of the New York Stock Exchange, whose family summered in Stockbridge, imported a marble fountain from Italy (later known fondly as the Cat and Dog Fountain) to adorn a triangular park at the intersection of South and Main Streets. The Stockbridge Library, which remains a private institution, was largely the work of LHA member John Z. Goodrich. No doubt encouraged by his wife, Goodrich donated the capital funds for the building after the LHA had

View toward town, 1860s. Courtesy Stockbridge Library Museum & Archives.

received a bequest of $2,000 for a town library from a former resident. In this case, the LHA took credit for the project, though the entire undertaking was a community effort. As a conduit for donors of civic structures, the association transformed the village of Stockbridge. Its success, particularly in these early years, was due to the leadership's personal generosity and ability to motivate associates in the ongoing effort to fund prioritized projects.[28]

On the LHA's tenth birthday, members took stock of their accomplishments of the past decade. Now the association functioned as a municipal organization, working with the town to achieve its vision. The town selectmen collaborated with members on several initiatives—installing the fence around the cemetery; repairing the footbridge and street crossings using wood cleared from Laurel Hill; and draining Main Street properly so that pedestrians could walk in both directions without "being set afloat."[29] In partnership with the Episcopal Society, the LHA transformed an unattractive corner opposite the hotel into a park. The association was quick to realize that such "harmony of action" was essential to its "aesthetical operations." After collaborating with "municipal fathers" on war-time projects, the association gained their confidence and finally felt regarded "as bona fide improvers and not mere administrators of whimsies and fancies."[30]

While the nation began the process of recovering from war, the association launched a range of long-term projects. Rev. Nathaniel Hillyer Egleston would work with Mary Hopkins Goodrich and J. E. Field as a member of the new committee on naming streets.[31] Looking forward, it was voted that Field obtain a deed for the Laurel Hill property from the Sedgwick family; Mrs. Ashburner's gift of a sidewalk between the River Bridge and the Railroad Station; and deeds of trust for the old Indian burying ground and a neighboring lot. Plans were made to plant trees on every road leading out of town, an improvement intended to create a "canopy of verdure" and enhance the village's reputation abroad as a summer retreat.[32] Members were confident of success now that they had the means for paying for it, thanks to an anticipated bequest of as much as $3,500 from longtime LHA member Abby D. Woodbridge.

The association continued its efforts to secure the burial ground, and the town erected a soldiers' monument in the small park at the intersection of Pine and Main Streets, soon to be known as Monument Square. The obelisk, topped by an eagle perched on a ball, was decorated with crossed swords and inscribed

"Willow Arch (a Berkshire roadway), Stockbridge," c. 1900–1915. Library of Congress Prints and Photographs Division.

Soldiers' Monument and Red Lion Inn, n.d. Postcard.

with the names of Stockbridge's twenty-eight fallen soldiers. Mary Hopkins Goodrich donated a corner lot to the Episcopal church, with the stipulation it remain "open ground" on behalf of the monument. The association wisely took on the responsibility of maintenance.[33] As town spaces were further clarified, more attention was paid to establishing connections between major destinations, such as a much-needed sidewalk from the railroad station southward, regrading walkways, and the seemingly endless work of replacing dead trees and planting new ones. To this end, the association appointed a member to request that the town adopt a recent Massachusetts law protecting shade trees bordering highways.[34]

Stockbridge Library, n.d. Postcard.

FOUR

IMPROVING THE NATION'S VILLAGES BY EXAMPLE

When Birdsey Grant Northrop delivered the keynote address at Anniversary Day in 1868, he was well known to many members of the audience. A Yale graduate, Congregational minister, and secretary of the Connecticut board of education, he frequently participated in Teachers' Institutes, where he was part of a circle that included Mark Hopkins. During the first week of August, Northrop attended the thirty-ninth annual meeting of the American Institute of Instruction in Pittsfield, from there traveling to Stockbridge, where he spoke before the annual gathering on Laurel Hill.[1]

A few months afterward, Northrop published "How to Make a Town Beautiful" in *Hearth and Home,* a new magazine dedicated to country life. His effort to promote village improvement societies drew on the success of the exemplary Stockbridge association. Members had planted more than 3,500 trees and improved the "sidewalks, streets, the public and private grounds" of the village. In addition to cultivating the taste of residents and promoting public spirit and good fellowship, the association boosted the local economy. "Every house, every building lot, every acre of land in the village" had increased in value since the LHA began its work. Now throngs of summer visitors filled the hotels and strolled along the tree-lined sidewalks of Main Street. Recently, Stockbridge had begun to attract wealthy families with powerful connections who sought idyllic country settings for their summer estates.[2]

Northrop also captured the LHA's sense of community spirit with descriptions of its efforts to elevate the public through education and monitoring of village behavior. The yearly meeting on Laurel Hill served to "fraternize the people, bringing together all classes on common ground, where differences of political or religious opinions were forgotten." The well-maintained landscape exemplified the association's good work. Monetary prizes encouraged extensive tree planting in public ways, and rewards were offered for evidence leading to the apprehension of vandals who dared damage fences, sidewalks, footbridges, or other improvements. The gift of the Stockbridge Library, free of cost to all, was the best example of how "these efforts to beautify the town have promoted general culture, as well as taste and public spirit." In his view, women played a special role in shaping such societies, for it was "a prominent lady of Stockbridge, then unmarried, to whose taste and efficiency the great and growing influence of this association is largely due." Northrop's article expanded the parameters of what had been seen as a local phenomenon by showing how the LHA's strategy could become a model for national progress. If Stockbridge's beauty was considered unique to a New England culture and landscape, Northrop suggested that villages across the country could adjust its organizational methods to suit their own communities.[3]

The association attributed increased interest in its activities to the "character of permanency" instilled by Abby Woodbridge's legacy, as well as notices in "influential periodicals of the country" written by visitors over the last sixteen years. Northrop was singled out for his work as a "public educator," who "preached the duty of every municipality to render its precincts beautiful, always pointing to Stockbridge as the model of how to do it." Since the publication of his article, states throughout the country, from Maine to Missouri, had requested copies of the LHA's constitution in the hope of launching similar organizations.[4]

Bolstered by this wave of national support, the LHA saw itself in a new light, as an exemplar worthy of emulation, and even invoked its own translation of the inscription on the British architect Sir Christopher Wren's tomb—"Stranger, if thou wouldst see his monument, look around!"—to emphasize its accomplishments. The association asked to be judged by "its *doings,*" and let these achievements "write its commentary."[5] The most dramatic recent accomplishment was the illumination of the village with gas streetlamps. George W. Brandon, a New York City resident who summered in Stockbridge and admired the association's work, had donated thirty oil lanterns. Unfortunately, only "irregular" light was shed, owing to the lack of a responsible caretaker. In later years, the association oversaw additional streetlamp installations, eventually illuminating the village center with more than fifty lanterns. Residents and visitors enjoyed the safety and comfort of well-lit streets, an amenity typically lacking in rural villages.

In 1870 the association announced that its "aesthetic progeny" now rivaled "the lineal descendants of the great Edwards, shortly expected to . . . commemorate their illustrious ancestor."[6] The Edwards family reunion, a long-anticipated event, was a particular honor to Stockbridge, the site chosen as most significant for the occasion. As the *New York Times* reported, "This beautiful town, nestled among the Berkshire hills, is all excitement over the great event of next week."[7] The article documented the "distinguished divine's" history, noting his renowned works prepared in Stockbridge, and predicted that at least a thousand descendants would soon assemble in the village. During the reunion, relatives planned a memorial to Edwards and solicited funds for it. By the next spring, a stone column supporting an urn was on order from Scotland, "another attraction" adding to Stockbridge's "beautiful locality."[8] In the meantime, the LHA planted eleven trees at the proposed site—the intersection of Church and West Main Streets—between the cemetery and village green.[9]

The remarkable municipal power of the LHA was perhaps best demonstrated by the authority it had to name the town's streets. In 1869 a committee of three longtime residents had been selected to lead the effort. New names included South Street, Pine Street, Prospect Street, Shamrock Lane, Vine Street, East Street, and Mill Street.[10] Poverty Lane became Church Street and Hammer Street was rechristened Elm Street. The committee's choice to replace "The Plain," a local term dating back to the first colonial settlement, with Main Street also suggests the group's desire for more refined public spaces. Two years after settling on the names, the LHA would show its powerful municipal hand again by designing, commissioning, and installing the town's first set of street signs.

At this point, the association revisited the idea of sponsoring a memorial to the Stockbridge Indians—likely owing to Mary Hopkins Goodrich. Now that

"Jonathan Edwards Monument, Town Hall, Children's Chimes, and Congregational Church, Stockbridge," n.d. Postcard.

the monument to Stockbridge's fallen soldiers was in place, and the great New England theologian's memorial was on its way, the LHA was ready to consider commemorating the "interesting tribe who were once the possessors of these mountains and vallies."[11] The memorial would demonstrate that the community had not forgotten its origins or the half century of shared associations that now existed merely as place names and stories. From this distance, LHA members could cherish the "quaint traditions" and "rude virtues" of the now absent tribe.[12] Goodrich and her cohort continued to advocate for the creation of a lasting memorial to the Stockbridge Mohicans for the next eight years.

•

Since moving to Stockbridge in 1860, Nathaniel Egleston had become increasingly involved in supporting the association's mission and promoting its influence throughout the nation. Having lived in New Haven and Hartford, and served parishes in Brooklyn, New York, and Madison, Wisconsin, the Congregational minister appreciated the benefits of country life.[13] Egleston's 1871 article for *Harper's New Monthly Magazine,* "A New England Village," showed how the Laurel Hill Association caused "art and taste to lend a helping hand to nature." In addition to extoling the town's well-maintained sidewalks, shade trees, and tidy public spaces, Egleston praised the LHA's encouragement of "a spirit of taste" among townspeople. Anniversary Days, which he considered key to motivating such refined work, were described in detail. After the association secretary read the "record of its doings for the past year," the election of officers took place, followed by an oration and often a poem. Members then made impromptu speeches to inspire the group's work over the next year.[14] *Harper's* circulated widely, and Egleston's article further spread the news of wonders wrought in Stockbridge by the Laurel Hill Association.

Despite the desire to maintain the village's charm, LHA members were conscious of the need to modernize as situations dictated. In 1873 the town replaced "the unsightly and unsafe old red bridge" crossing the Housatonic west of the village with a "massive iron structure," known as "Tuckerman's Bridge." Members approved construction that seemed safer and more refined, praising the town for its "its spirit of improvement."[15] Nevertheless, the LHA hoped that the "additional front" to the high school building, currently under construction, would prove worthy of "its charming locality and the demands of public sentiment."[16]

The association increasingly saw itself as contributing to the industrial age by manufacturing community spirit and civic responsibility. Its annual report for 1874 articulated the economic value of the Laurel Hill Association's work to the town by noting that "the external beautifying of the place would enhance the value of real estate, and that the outlay of money for this purpose would prove a

Tuckerman's Bridge, c. 1905–1915. Library of Congress Prints and Photographs Division.

more profitable instrument than the same amount in Bank or Railroad stocks, or the best bond and mortgage securities." Both residents and visitors were informed of the emotional and economic reasons for supporting the LHA. Looking back from its twenty-one years of experience, the group proclaimed success in having "won for Stockbridge the reputation of a model town for beauty throughout the land." Anniversary Day that year included performances from the Stockbridge Musical Band and the Hampton Singers, Samuel Chapman Armstrong's Black choral group from the Hampton Normal and Agricultural Institute in Hampton, Virginia.[17]

In their efforts to further village improvement nationally, Egleston and Northrop crossed paths with other leaders in the movement to bring sanitation to rural locations. One champion of the cause, the engineer George E. Waring, launched his career working for Frederick Law Olmsted and became an international authority on sanitation. Beginning in the mid-1870s, Waring wrote on village improvement and sanitary work for *Scribner's Monthly: An Illustrated Magazine for the People,* promoting the Laurel Hill Association and Stockbridge's unparalleled progress in this respect. His article resulted in a flood of "letters from every part of the country wishing for information [on village improvement societies]—the latest from the interior of Texas. . . . What the beginners want—literally by the thousands—is to know just how to do it."[18] In 1877, Waring collected his *Scribner's* articles and two essays on farm communities in *Village Improvements and Farm Villages*. Both *Scribner's* and the book included a copy of a constitution for a village improvement society, "suggested by the regulations governing the Laurel Hill Association of Stockbridge."[19] Reprinting the LHA constitution proved the most effective method of furthering the movement.

A new map of Stockbridge published in 1876 illustrates the breadth of the LHA's power over the character, landscape, and identity of the town. The public parks are rendered in green, indicating that such spaces were becoming significant features of the town, and all the streets are named. The moral uplift of the group's influence was less tangible, but equally important. When new benches installed on Main Street attracted some "rowdy" loafers, "gentlemen who have known this village for many years . . . heard more profanity, vulgarity and noise in the streets than ever before." Fearing that such behavior might damage Stockbridge's reputation and lower property values, the association reminded members that every "civilized person hates with a profound hatred . . . senseless and vulgar noise, and civilized society everywhere protects itself against it."[20] Members clearly articulated their belief in the value of maintaining propriety throughout the village. The LHA's allies in this effort were "residents from abroad among us" who erected "abodes of taste and refinement."[21]

In the months before the LHA anniversary celebration in 1878, Nathaniel Egleston introduced the association and its work to a wider audience through *Villages and Village Life with Hints for Their Improvement*. His influential book strove both to motivate citizens in the preservation of rural traditions and to offer practical suggestions for village beautification. A review in the *Chicago Daily Tribune* identified the most interesting chapters as "those which treat of Village Improvement Societies, the Laurel Hill Association, Trees, and Tree-Planting, Fences and Hedges, and the Sanitary Aspects of Country Life."[22] Egleston described how the association's ability to organize volunteers and educate villagers in tasteful stewardship had made the "Stockbridge of to-day quite a different place from the Stockbridge of twenty, or even of ten, years ago."[23]

Egleston dedicated *Villages and Village Life* to Andrew Jackson Downing, and his ideas about country homes recall Downing's writings on the subject. The clergyman advocated for sweeping lawns uninterrupted by fences, well-planted trees, and tidy yards—indications of maintenance associated with moral virtues. Hard work, frugality, and simplicity guaranteed a cultured, ethical society. For these reasons, village homes were "precious" to the nation.[24] He assured his readers that "there can be no dispute about women's rights here," offering women authority in "matters of taste and feeling." A section of the book devoted to the "refining influences of women" emphasized the importance of both sexes working together on behalf of village improvement. Although described only as a village "in mind," Stockbridge is clearly the model exemplifying the excellent work "done largely through the instrumentality of women." In Stockbridge, he observed, "the gentler sex have borne a conspicuous part" in all "councils."[25]

The twenty-fifth anniversary of the Laurel Hill Association was marked by a tribute to its founder, a passionate account remarkably different from the speeches of past celebrations, which were typically focused on municipal achievements. Now in her mid-sixties, Goodrich was extolled as the inspiration behind the cause. It was recalled how, while on horseback, she interviewed "the professional man at his studies; the merchant behind his counter; the mechanic in his shop; the farmer in his field and even the children on their way to and from school," preaching the "gospel of aesthetics" and urging her audiences to join her in making "Stockbridge the paradise of towns—the joy of the earth." This public recognition may have been related to Goodrich's many successes over the past year: she had arranged for the cemetery stones to be adjusted and cleaned, persuaded the executive committee to organize a group devoted to the monument in the Indian Burial Ground, and secured a donation for an inscription memorializing the Sedgwick family's gift of Laurel Hill. The rock behind the rostrum was to be inscribed "Laurel Hill—Sedgwick gift to Stockbridge, 1834."[26]

Through her example, Goodrich furthered the association's tradition of receiving bequests from private citizens. Sometimes monetary, these gifts were more often municipal art items or land for use in public projects guided by the association. David Dudley Field donated a memorial structure, later known as the Children's Chime Tower. At the annual Anniversary Day celebration, Goodrich marked the culmination of her nearly decade-long effort to sponsor a memorial to the Stockbridge Indians. A natural obelisk, cut by lightning from a rock ledge in Ice Glen and dragged to the site by six horses, the monument was payment of "a long-standing debt to an interesting and fast-fading people."[27]

The following year Rev. Jeremiah Slingerland, a Mohican sachem and minister to the Stockbridge-Munsee Community in Wisconsin, was invited to deliver the keynote address at Anniversary Day.[28] Newspapers reported on Slingerland's upcoming talk and the expected attendance of the first Indigenous members of the Hampton Institute, who were spending the summer with farmers in Lee. The Mohicans were most likely responsible for attracting a crowd of nearly a thousand, the largest Anniversary Day attendance to date.[29]

Slingerland's address outlined the history of his tribe, from their early years along the Housatonic to their life in Stockbridge, participation in the Revolutionary War, and migration in search of a new homeland. He assured the audience that his people "take pleasure and rejoice in the beautifying and improvement" of village homes and "this entire place, because it was the former home of their fathers as well as yours. And when it was announced that your good society had erected so gigantic a monument over the graves of their forefathers, and a vote of thanks was offered, every head was uplifted, every eye brightened, and every face covered with smiles."[30] Slingerland concluded by predicting that the tribe would disband, like others before them, and become assimilated into the United States, a future he declared not only was for the best but was the fulfillment of prophecy.[31]

By the end of the decade, in part because of its growing celebrity as a civic organization, the Laurel Hill Association began to take on more ambitious advocacy projects. Members proposed that the Massachusetts legislature adopt a weed ordinance based on the State of New York's recent statute "concerning the nuisances from weeds, brambles, etc. on lands abutting upon public highways." The association's committee on parks and squares was given the charge of drafting

Field Memorial Chimes, n.d. Postcard.

Rev. Jeremiah Slingerland at LHA dedication of Burying Ground Monument, 1879. Courtesy Stockbridge Library Museum & Archives.

a bill for a similar law in Massachusetts and lobbying for it at the next session of the legislature. Although the statute was "killed—apparently by the pressure of other (though scarcely less important) schemes of reform," the LHA continued to expand its efforts as stewards of the regional landscape.[32]

Beginning in 1880, the association addressed the growing threat of malaria in the Connecticut and Housatonic valleys. In some cases, the danger had been attributed to the shade from trees, and the LHA recognized that its own "arborific darlings" might have to confront "ruthless surgery to the point where aesthetics and safety may wed and be happy." When the selectmen were slow to act on wetland areas—"malarial ditches"—near the railroad station, the LHA appealed directly to the state, threatening to take the case to court if the public health hazard remained unresolved. The threat of a lawsuit secured the railroad commission's attention, and the association received a letter stating that the ditches would be addressed during the construction of a new railroad station.[33]

Following this success, the LHA tried to get an article put on the town meeting warrant for the creation of a town board of health. This effort failed, however, as town officials argued that residents would never pass such an ordinance.[34] The association's forays into public health and welfare were motivated by an increasing understanding of the importance of sanitation in rural communities. The founding in 1882 of the National Association for Sanitary and Rural Improvement in Greenwood Lake, New York, reflected this element in the general push to improve American life.

In a paper written for its first organizational meeting, the widely known sanitary reform pioneer Harriette Merrick Plunkett, author of *Women, Plumbers, and Doctors; or, Household Sanitation,* turned to Mary Hopkins's story to demonstrate the importance of women in the reform effort. A native of Pittsfield, Plunkett was an early promoter of women's involvement in municipal sanitation. She described how Hopkins had transformed Stockbridge through "village adornment," reasoning that if one woman could achieve such perfection, then certainly women's work was crucial to a national sanitary organization.[35] The LHA had become a model not only for municipalities throughout the nation but also for volunteer organizations dedicated to improving sanitation and rural life.

•

New England: A Handbook for Travelers, first published in 1873, described the LHA as "devoted to preserving, protecting, and increasing the beauty of the village and its environs," a mission that now served to advertise Stockbridge's charm to outsiders.[36] Increasingly the estates of the founding families, highly regarded for their heritage and refined appearance, were being rented out over the summer, and many tenants came to build summer homes of their own around the village center. There was a growing consciousness of Stockbridge's unique character and interest to travelers. The selectmen noted Stockbridge's "many attractions, not the least of which are its good roads and pleasant drives, which should be kept in good order," and the Laurel Hill Association responded by shifting its focus from municipal planning toward scenic preservation of the village center.[37]

As the resort-town economy grew, debate over the "conflict between commerce and aesthetics" gained momentum. In spring 1884, Charles Rathburn, a gravestone cutter, and Nelson Weeks, a mason, began selling small land parcels subdivided from a larger property abutting Main Street and extending north. The thirty-by-fifteen-foot lots were priced at two to four hundred dollars, affordable to lower-income residents, some of whom lived on the old "Poverty Lane." Soon word spread that bids had been received for the lots fronting Main Street,

"In the Housatonic Valley—Stockbridge in the Berkshires," n.d. Postcard.

Lenox Road and Stockbridge Bowl, 1899. Photo by Arthur Wentworth Scott from John Coleman Adams, *Nature Studies in Berkshire*. The Clark Digital Collections.

across from the Sedgwick estate. The interested parties were a blacksmith, a livery operator, and a mortician.[38]

The Sedgwick family and other Main Street property owners felt threatened by such "commerce" near their homes. A group of residents, headed by Henry Sedgwick, mobilized to purchase the property through collected subscriptions. By July nearly five thousand dollars had been pledged to the cause, far more than was needed to purchase the two small plots. Subscribers planned to buy the property, develop it as a private social club, and prevent unwanted businesses from locating in the village center. On July 11, 1884, Sedgwick held the first official meeting of the newly assembled Stockbridge Casino Company at his home. The Company proposed building a structure for social gatherings, open only to Casino Company subscribers and their guests. New residents would find an appropriate social circle at the Casino. When it opened in 1888, the club posted its "rules of admission of subscribers and visitors." Those with proper credentials could enjoy its tennis courts, billiard tables, theatrical productions, and social gatherings.[39]

Another indication of Stockbridge's growing wealth was the replacement in 1884 of the original wooden Gothic Revival Episcopal church, considered monumental when Richard Upjohn designed it in the 1840s, with a building of local Berkshire granite designed in the popular Richardsonian Romanesque style by Charles F. McKim. While the new St. Paul's was going up at the corner of Main and Pine Streets, a town office building was constructed across the street. The fireproof, red-brick Dutch Colonial building would house the offices of the board of selectmen, the police, and the town clerk. The town's investment in its

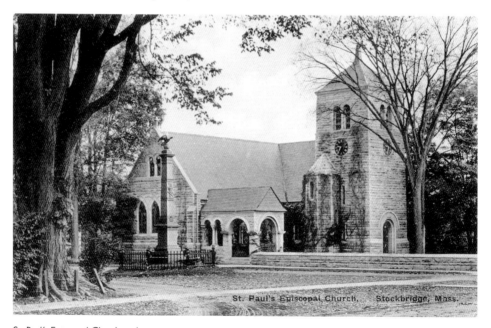

St. Paul's Episcopal Church, n.d. Postcard.

governance and the gift of the new church (Charles Butler provided the funding in memory of his wife, Susan Ridley Sedgwick Butler, and McKim donated his services), further enhanced the village center.

In August 1885, about a year after the initial discussion of the Casino site, the property was deeded to Prescott Hall Butler, who was to hold it in legal trust. Although the Laurel Hill Association appears not to have had any official role in the founding of the Stockbridge Casino Company, several subscribers were active members, and Henry Sedgwick served as president of both organizations simultaneously. The association's annual report, read aloud at Anniversary Day, included a lengthy discussion of the purchase of "a lot on Main Street . . . by clubbed subscription of several residents and property holders." The action suggested a "conflict between commerce and aesthetics" and evoked strong opinions.

Sedgwick and others involved in the founding of the Stockbridge Casino framed their concerns over unwanted businesses on Main Street within the larger discussion of village development. Blacksmith shops, funeral homes, and liveries would have contributed to a year-round merchant-based economy, but they did not belong in a village primarily identified as a summer resort. The association described its improvements as exemplifying "the element of beauty, generously bestowed by nature and successfully cultivated by art through many years of labor," and asserted that when this ideal came "in conflict with business, the latter (unless a positive necessity) should unhesitatingly give way to the former."[40] In a region of dying farms and increasing commercial growth, this statement reflected larger concerns about securing the future of Stockbridge center

Village Green with Cat and Dog Fountain, n.d. Postcard.

as a nonindustrial village landscape. Before the purchase of the Casino property, the LHA had not publicly approved of any actions in the community which advanced the interests of part-time residents and visitors over those of Stockbridge citizens. Now the association had created a village with qualities that attracted tourism, and it recognized the importance of protecting its investment.

By purchasing the Casino property and preventing "unseemly" businesses on Main Street, Sedgwick's group instituted unofficial zoning. The Casino founders also clarified the town's priorities for future land use development based on the tradition of large estates and their requirements: clipped lawns, ample street trees, raked gravel pedestrian walks, and an overall air of tidiness and refinement. Within a span of four decades, Stockbridge had been comprehensively planned through innovative municipal work, planting, and social programming. The Laurel Hill Association now served primarily as guardian of the decorous village.

•

Beginning in the late 1880s, visits to the Berkshires by socialites and prominent families were regularly announced in society columns of the *New York Times* and the *Boston Globe.* Village social and sporting events, weddings, and other celebrations also received notice. Neglected farmland suddenly was transformed by wealthy urban visitors, or, as a journalist for the *St. Albans Daily Messenger* enthused, "The advent of the 'summer boarder' has caused the 'desert' of the last decade to bloom as a rose garden. The abandoned farm house has become a 'summer cottage,' whose picturesqueness delights the trained eye of an artist. . . . Blessed be the summer visitor in the highways and byways of rural Massachusetts!" Reflecting back on this time with a mix of sadness and pride, the novelist Nathalie Sedgwick Colby recalled that the "outside was slowly creeping into the village. Summer people were buying places. . . . Down the street the big family of Joseph H. Choate were going to build on a hill. . . . The Matthew Arnolds took the house where the Musgraves used to give us supper on the lawn."[41] Generally these new homes were larger and more opulent than the established old family estates.

Elm Court, a cottage designed by the architecture firm Peabody & Stearns for William Douglas Sloane and Emily Thorn Vanderbilt, exemplified the trend. The largest Shingle-style house in America, the grand residence stood on the boundary between Stockbridge and its neighbor Lenox, an indication of the close relationship between the two summer retreats, and of their differences. Lenox would become known for "Swiss Chalets, Tudor and Elizabethan castles," rising on "the astonished slopes of the hills," while Stockbridge operated at a slower pace and favored a smaller scale.[42] Summer visitors often moved between the two. A reviewer for the *Nation* recognized the "symbiotic" relationship of the

"Elm Court, country home of W. D. Sloane, Lenox," c. 1910–1920. Library of Congress Prints and Photographs Division.

Mark Hopkins House, Stockbridge, 1935. Library of Congress Prints and Photographs Division.

villages, commenting that their "geographical and social boundaries or dividing lines are not precisely coincident, and some residents whose houses are in one township are socially at home in the other."[43] During the frenzy of cottage construction along the Stockbridge border, the Laurel Hill Association focused on maintaining the village's natural charm and emphasizing its virtuous citizenry.

This growing civic consciousness was enhanced by coverage in popular media of Stockbridge's many attributes. A journalist for the *Boston Herald* called Stockbridge "unique—the neatest, most orderly, and best kept town that I have ever seen in the country." Even more significant, he remarked on how the place instilled in its visitors an enthusiasm for the village's character, pulling them into its aura. When he carelessly tossed away a bit of paper, "it was instantly apparent," lying "on the close cropped emerald stubble," looking "as if it could be seen for ten miles. I picked it up and carried it to the waste basket; there was no other way." Another writer remarked in the *New York Times* that, although all Berkshire towns were "fresh and clean and wholesome," Stockbridge was most obviously "the model village." There, "even the humblest of the villagers' homes are painted and scoured and vine-covered and embowered" with cultivated flowers, shrubs, and trees.[44]

The refined landscape molded by the Laurel Hill Association made the village famous, and Stockbridge likewise gained renown as the birthplace of the first and most successful village improvement society in the nation. While many New England towns were welcoming industry, Stockbridge was praised for its lack of factories and predominance of well-maintained trees and open space. Without embracing economic development, it had become a modern model of aesthetic progress, community cohesion, sanitation, and cleanliness.

Throughout this prosperous time, the LHA helped usher in the type of development that would retain the village aesthetic. For the design of the Casino, the new showpiece on Main Street, Joseph Choate recommended his friend Charles McKim. The prominent New York firm McKim, Mead & White was completing Choate's summer home, Naumkeag, on the hill overlooking Main Street. In 1887, while the Casino was under construction, a land company purchased 1,100 acres around Stockbridge Bowl, the lake just north of the village center, with the plan to improve the property and sell it off in large parcels for grand residential estates.[45] The grandest of these was Shadow Brook, a hundred-room Tudor Revival mansion built for the wealthy merchant Anson Phelps Stokes and his family. Overlooking the Bowl, surrounded by "a bewildering array" of fields and forests, mountains and valleys," Shadow Brook was one of the largest houses in America when it was completed in 1893.[46] The property engulfed Samuel Ward's old summer home, Oakwood, which Stokes had converted into stables.

A growing number of such extensive family estates functioned as working

Naumkeag, entrance from the southeast, 1885. Library of Congress Prints and Photographs Division.

Shadow Brook, n.d. Postcard.

"Memorial Bridge, Stockbridge," 1906. Postcard.

"The Ice Glen, Stockbridge," c. 1910–1920. Library of Congress Prints and Photographs Division.

farms and required large staffs to care for residents, buildings, gardens, and vehicles. Stokes owned "the finest of registered stock" and during the winter received daily orders of dairy, produce, and meat at his New York City home. In the Berkshires, "a small army" harvested crops into November and maintained the greenhouses.[47] Many other wealthy families, including the Choates, had their Stockbridge staffs make regular shipments of perishables via the Housatonic Railroad to their winter homes in New York.[48] The construction of the enormous Stokes estate within the pristine landscape of the Stockbridge Bowl must have seemed shocking to longtime residents, but the sophisticated leaders of the Laurel Hill Association saw it as a sign of the times.

Mary Hopkins Goodrich, "the most unremitting promotor of the Laurel Hill Association," embodied the group's progressive spirit. Still vigorous at eighty years old, Goodrich was keen to expand the trail system around Laurel Hill, beginning with construction of a bridge that would give pedestrians access not only to the forty-acre parcel known as Ice Glen, donated to the association by David Dudley Field, but also to its surrounding landscape. Having already approved plans and estimates for the project, she hoped to see it carried out in her lifetime and according to her specifications.[49] The new bridge was to be of modern design, featuring a reinforced concrete arch, very different from the metal truss bridge it replaced.[50] In January 1895 her plans were approved and construction contracted. She died the following month.[51]

In their eulogy, members of the association spoke of her formative role in kindling the civic beautification movement throughout the nation.

> Laurel Hill, so far back as 1834 had been the gift of the Sedgwick family to the town. That gift lent impetus to the spirit of village improvement, and that spirit, under the leadership and enthusiasm of Mrs. Goodrich— then Miss Hopkins—took definite shape in the organization in 1853 of the Laurel Hill Association. That Association, and the results of its work, are her enduring monument. . . . Nor since this Association is the parent of all village improvement societies in the United States, has her influence ended here. . . . Through these multitudinous societies the good work to which in the Berkshires she gave the impulse, today helps brighten and beautify the whole land.[52]

Mary Hopkins Goodrich was buried in the Stockbridge Cemetery in a grave facing John Konkapot's, not far from the memorial to his ancestors.

"Main Street, elms, Stockbridge," c. 1905–1915. Library of Congress Prints and Photographs Division.

FIVE

A TWENTIETH-CENTURY VILLAGE

In 1893 the fortieth anniversary of the Laurel Hill Association coincided with the final months of the World's Columbian Exhibition in Chicago, but the tens of thousands of visitors exploring the dazzling "White City" could hardly have been expected to connect the Laurel Hill Association with this Beaux-Arts display of American innovation and urban planning. A few years later, however, the author Mary Caroline Robbins traced the origins of the new City Beautiful movement to Stockbridge's Laurel Hill Association. In a series of articles for the *Atlantic Monthly,* Robbins painted a vivid picture of how the association had perfected its village, a model of local progress for the next century. Now, she observed, the country needed to focus on improving its rapidly growing cities, the exemplars of "the higher civilization." Village improvement was a catalyst for launching the new technologies and planning methods of the era.[1]

When the *Boston Globe* reported on the popularity of village improvement—from Maine to California—the focus was on encouraging volunteer work as a means of elevating local culture. The Laurel Hill Association not only respected the "natural, wild beauty" of its village, and honored regional history with a monument to the Indians, but it also meticulously maintained the town's infrastructure by keeping driveways smooth and hard, maintaining a sidewalk system throughout the village, and sending out a sprinkler to keep the dust down in summer and a snow plow to clear the streets in winter. The diligent efforts of the association appeared to have effectively reduced poverty (leaving the curious to wonder where the poor people lived). This laudable achievement was underscored by increased property values of between 20 and 50 percent, certainly an incentive to inspire further emulation.[2]

"On the Housatonic, Stockbridge," n.d. New York Public Library Digital Collections.

In 1899 the botanist, conservationist, and reform leader Mira Lloyd Dock, speaking about civic beautification at the International Conference of Women in London, traced the "local" form of village improvement to "Miss Hopkins of Stockbridge," whose work had become "a model for hundreds of others in all parts of our country." Inspired by the efforts she saw in England and Europe, Dock became an active proponent of city beautification and led the campaign to beautify her native Harrisburg, Pennsylvania. She understood the importance of public parks both for beauty and for health and, on a larger scale, the need to protect forests and large tracts of land. She pointed to Massachusetts, which in 1891 had established The Trustees of Public Reservations, and to "a national Park and Outdoor Art Association," founded in Louisville, Kentucky, in 1897, now leading the way in acquiring and conserving land throughout the nation.[3] The Laurel Hill Association was first in her chronological list of "notable organizations" in conservation, including the National Park Service, Arbor Day, the Appalachian Mountain Club, and the American Scenic and Historic Preservation Society.[4] Throughout her career, Dock would continue to connect village improvement work with park making and forest conservation.

At the turn of the century, Jessie M. Good, "Florist & Seedswoman" of Springfield, Ohio, also looked to the model of Stockbridge. In a series of articles on village improvement published by *How to Grow Flowers* magazine, she recounts how the Laurel Hill Association's transformation of its village inspired the many improvement societies that had sprung up around the country. The National League of Improvement Associations, founded in 1900 at a convention in Springfield she had organized, launched a nationwide conversation among "organizations interested in the permanent improvement and beautifying of American homes and their surroundings whether in country, village or city."[5]

In mid-August 1901, following the Pan-American Exposition, the National League of Improvement Associations held its second annual convention in Buffalo. Drawing together leaders in housing reform, the American Park and Outdoor Art Association, and the League of American Wheelmen—a national organization of bicyclists who advocated for the improvement of roads and highways—the convention reflected the differences between the early village beautification movement and the mobilization for civic improvement in the early twentieth century. The shift from local, volunteer-based efforts to urban-centered, expert-driven programs could be seen in the renaming of the League as the American League for Civic Improvement and its instituting a professional membership for landscape gardeners, manufacturers, architects, contractors, and other businessmen.[6] Jessie Good prepared *The Work of Civic Improvement* and *The How of Civic Improvement,* manuals from which organizations could draw ideas and inspiration. The American League sold these publications and others, including *The Improvement of Towns and Cities* by Charles Mulford Robinson.[7] Prepared lectures illustrated with lantern slides were made available, and community members could request presentation by a league board member.[8]

Leaders in civic improvement praised the Laurel Hill Association as the model but viewed the organization in the context of a new era. In a 1902 article for the *Century Magazine,* Sylvester Baxter, secretary of the Massachusetts Metropolitan Park Commission, described the LHA's activities in detail, with the goal of emphasizing the "vastly greater results" to be achieved by the next generation. The same year, in the *Chautauquan,* Charles Zueblin, secretary of the American League for Civic Improvement, cited the LHA as the founding improvement association but declared the last decade as the most important in terms of bettering American life. Both men referred to new groups that were contributing to the progress: the National League of Improvement Associations, now the American League for Civic Improvement, and the General Federation of Women's Clubs. Zueblin, inspired by the example of the McMillan Commission, saw great promise in urban planning. Now, he believed, "no city should be content with anything less than a comprehensive plan." As Baxter pointed out, the goals for the new era of civic improvement were grounded in principles put forward by the LHA—aesthetic taste, public health, community cooperation, all leading "toward the ideals of a higher civilization." The Laurel Hill Association had set the standard fifty years earlier, but it and its kindred organizations now needed to learn from twentieth-century planners.[9]

•

In January 1901 a railway company was making plans to build a trolley line extending in a north–south route through Berkshire County. The proposed trolley would travel through Sheffield, Great Barrington, Stockbridge, Lee, and Lenox on its way to Pittsfield, where another line headed to North Adams. Details about this development plan appeared in the *New York Times,* and concern spread quickly through the towns and among summer residents. Despite the general opinion that the main streets of Lenox and Stockbridge should be bypassed by the trolley lines, the selectmen of Lenox consulted "a number of the cottagers and prominent citizens" and ultimately granted the franchise for the trolley to the Berkshire Street Railway Company.[10]

In Stockbridge, however, because of the Laurel Hill Association and the population of loyal summer residents, the approval process for major initiatives was more complicated. By this time, summer residents were the major landholders in the village, owning nearly 75 percent of the farmland and forest within a one-mile radius of Main Street. Maintaining the pastoral charm of their summer homes soon became a priority.[11] The LHA quickly mustered its forces. Bainbridge Colby, a summer resident from New York who was later Woodrow Wilson's last secretary of state, made an impassioned speech to the association in the fall of 1901. He compared Stockbridge's fight to successful struggles in Cleveland, New York, Berlin, and other cities where excessive traffic had been diverted, the banks of waterways worked into parks, and dangerous rail crossings prevented. He firmly believed that "the great though unorganized sentiment in Massachusetts of respect for nature . . . should be appealed to" in the effort to protect the state's "remaining places of beauty." With a nod to the association, he argued that community leaders could control the installation of modern innovations so that beauty and peace were not lost amid the progressive trends of civilization. Stockbridge's "Fight for an Avenue" was not simply a struggle to maintain the patronage of summer visitors, but a battle against the interests of the masses who lacked foresight.[12]

A lengthy article in the *New York Times* demonstrated widespread support for preserving a place in which community spirit was reflected in the landscape. Stockbridge was the most beautiful village in the Berkshires, "an idyll in country life . . . its intense quiet . . . soothing to city folk, who enjoy to the full its magnificent aisles of boles and branches and the picturesqueness of its spacious ways." However, "into this Eden there [was] about to penetrate one of the noisiest of modern inventions, the trolley, a necessity in cities and a boon to the countryside, but an innovation ruinous to the pleasure given by grave and stately avenues of trees." Such devastation frequently occurred—decisions were made by state officials, not local townspeople. If Stockbridge gave in, "it would not be the first time that the ignorant killed the goose with the golden eggs."[13]

Ironically, the electric trolley was invented in Stockbridge by Stephen D. Field, who ardently opposed installing one in his hometown.[14]

•

The trolley was destined to connect Stockbridge to the network of Berkshire towns, a step forward many approved, but the battle to keep it off Main Street continued. In the meantime, an eighty-five-room hotel was constructed atop Prospect Hill. Opening in 1904, luxurious Heaton Hall overlooked the village, suggesting both the region's increasingly promising tourist trade and the need to secure its scenic legacy. During the early twentieth century, Stockbridge's wealthy summer residents continued to play a dominant role in the Laurel Hill Association. Joseph Choate, Secretary of the Navy C. J. Bonaparte, and Commissioner of Indian Affairs Francis E. Leupp all were involved in the LHA and had strong opinions about how modernization was altering their beloved place of respite.[15] This affluent population acted as village watchdogs, influencing public opinion in favor of policies that enhanced the improved

Heaton Hall, n.d. Postcard.

nineteenth-century landscape and taking measures to curb the negative effects of auto tourism and development. Stockbridge's social space continued to be controlled with as much precision as its infrastructure.

When the poor condition of a temporary trolley station became a concern, the LHA spoke with summer resident C. S. Mellen, president of the New York, New Haven & Hartford Railroad. A few months later Mellen joined the association, and reworking the station and its grounds became a topic of discussion.[16] Together with influential community members, the association formed the Society for the Protection of the Highways of Stockbridge to further the battle to keep the trolley off Main Street. The selectmen had negotiated with the trolley company and railroad commissioners on the cost of building the line just south of the village center, and although the local press described the group as a hindrance to progress, it had garnered pledges of $10,000 from residents to defray the additional expense.[17] By the end of the fight, that figure had risen to $25,000, the community groups were successful, and the LHA collaborated on helping the railroad proceed on purchasing and leasing the necessary property. Years later, the society's role was forgotten and the LHA primarily credited with rallying the community to prevent the trolley on Main Street. The victory became legendary, an inspiration in the association's later battles to preserve the town's character.

Throughout these years, the association continued its efforts to illuminate the village in an aesthetically pleasing manner. Since 1890 the town had appropriated funds for fuel and a lamplighter through an annual warrant voted on by residents.[18] In 1908, when electrifying the village was under consideration, the association voted to hand over full responsibility for street lighting to the town. The LHA owned the lanterns that would be electrified, which now numbered close to seventy gas and kerosene lamps, and later used this as leverage to lobby successfully for public support to place the unsightly wires underground.[19] As with the trolley, the LHA demonstrated its willingness to embrace progress that did not infringe on the beauty and integrity of Main Street. Its greatest challenge in this regard was yet to come.

•

In 1893 the first state highway commission in the United States was established in Massachusetts. Three commissioners appointed by the governor were given the authority and budget to oversee design, construction, and maintenance of state roads.[20] One of the commissioners, George A. Perkins, belonged to the League of American Wheelmen, which now had a membership of more than one hundred thousand, and over the next several years lobbied for systematic road improvements. In a piece for the *Boston Daily Globe,* he proclaimed that

"New England is the mecca for tourists" and argued for a "system of roads connecting mountains and lakes with the seashore," which would garner the state valuable revenue from tourism and roadside development.[21] Like many of his peers, Perkins championed motor "touring" as ideal for the modern wealthy vacationer, and soon society pages were announcing who was arriving in the Berkshires by car rather than train. The *New York Times* ran features detailing selected routes through New England, complete with road maps and snapshots of pastoral scenes taken from a car. The "beauties" of the Berkshires would "induce most tourists to tarry for a day or two to enjoy its good roads for short excursions."[22] Motoring was a hobby, a status symbol, and a declaration of embracing modern times.

To improve travel to and from the Berkshires, the Massachusetts Highway Commission completed several large-scale road-building projects, combined with scenic preservation of associated roadside viewsheds. Jacob's Ladder Trail, opened in 1910, was quickly followed by planning of the Mohawk Trail to run

"On the road to Stockbridge, Lenox," c. 1905–1915. Library of Congress Prints and Photographs Division.

along the original Indigenous trade route between Atlantic and upstate New York tribes. The new roads made it possible for travelers from Boston to drive to the Berkshires and return by a different route. Residents of Stockbridge both benefited from this increased visitation and were annoyed by the influx of traffic. By 1913, Main Street was described as "congested," and speeding, particularly on weekends, as "frightful." LHA members petitioned the town to install "speed law signs" in the village center and on another occasion build "curbings" on Main Street to prevent automobiles from driving off the road onto village land.[23]

The increase in tourism led to an initiative, promoted by the short-lived *Stockbridge* magazine, to develop a "local Baedeker," the publication of which would "most naturally be supplied by the Laurel Hill Association." Such a guidebook would illuminate the history of local landmarks and motivate both residents and visitors to explore the town's sites. Unlike a "rail-road" folder, the guide must aspire to some "literary permanency" and include descriptions with directions and the average time necessary to reach destinations, like the Appalachian Mountain Club's *White Mountain Guide.* Those intent on promoting Stockbridge as a "historic village" hoped to capitalize on their town's famous landscape, a cultural attraction in its own right.[24]

Members of the association had long considered trees essential to Stock-

"Watering Place along the Mohawk Trail in the Berkshires," 1917. Postcard.

bridge's beauty and character, but the condition of the trees along Main Street had been ignored for years. On behalf of the association, Elizabeth Bullard drew attention to this priority by writing to Frederick Law Olmsted Jr., requesting his guidance in replacing damaged trees and enhancing existing roadways with new plantings. After receiving no response, she asked her cousin, LHA member Bernhard Hoffmann, to follow up with another letter.[25] On October 7, 1914, Hoffman wrote to Olmsted, reminding him that they had once met briefly on a train and asking for his assistance in developing a "far sighted and well advised planting plan," with insight on selecting proper trees, spacing arrangements, and other details. A map had been prepared showing the location and "classification" of all the village trees.[26]

The firm responded immediately, promising to send an assistant to estimate costs for a report on "street planting in Stockbridge." Later that month, the landscape architect Harold Hill Blossom represented Olmsted Brothers at a meeting with the LHA tree committee. "A Report on the Improvement of the Town of Stockbridge" was submitted to the LHA on December 23, 1913. In March 1914 the majority of the report was published as a "special supplement" to the first issue of *Stockbridge*.[27] Ellen Eddy Shaw attributed the publication of this new monthly, edited by Walter Prichard Eaton, to the "stimulating" effects of the Laurel Hill Association, which was responsible for motivating the community to accept "progressive measures."

Over the next few years, Bernhard Hoffman continued his work for the LHA and his association with Harold Blossom. In the fall of 1916, when Walter H. Clarke donated land along the Housatonic to the association, Hoffman had the foresight to imagine the riverside parcel as part of a parklike setting enhancing the Stockbridge railroad station grounds. To this end, he secured Blossom's help in launching a plan for spring planting. The two had cultivated a friendship during their previous collaboration, and when Blossom visited the village, he left Hoffman a copy of the *American Magazine of Art* with an article he had written about Andrew Jackson Downing. A thank-you note from Hoffman expressed his pleasure in the gift and "delightful line of association with H.H.B."[28]

Olmsted Brothers created a grading plan and "proposed treatment of the station grounds," which outlined a drainage system and suggested building restrictions. The design anticipated considerable traffic, recommending a thirty-two-foot-wide driveway to accommodate four lines of moving vehicles. More aesthetic features included a footpath along the river, recommendations for tree planting, and a list of preferred native shrubs. By February 1917, LHA president Alexander Sedgwick accepted the plan, although Hoffman expressed the consensus that it seemed "almost hopeless to attempt any work in these trying

"R. R. Station, Stockbridge," n.d. Postcard.

days."[29] Two months later America entered World War I, and President Sedgwick soon left for the front.

•

Upon its completion in 1915, the Mohawk Trail was considered "undoubtedly the most important piece of highway work in this State and probably in the New England States in many years."[30] The road encouraged more auto tourists from Boston and coastal resorts to venture into the Berkshire Hills and experience the sense of wonder inspired by the vistas. From a "grand view platform" along the Trail, one took in "a view of valleys and mountains unsurpassed in the East in grandeur and surpassed nowhere in diversity of charm. City and country town, rich farm lands, silver streams, deep forest groves and the peaks of lesser hills lie at the feet of the observer."[31]

The new roads and increased tourism led to the proliferation of advertisements along roadsides. Within the village, the LHA monitored the issue, contacting residents when their signs violated local ordinances. In the summer of 1915 a ladies' tea room opened on Main Street and boldly placed its sign on the sidewalk. The LHA took immediate action, insisting that the proprietors move it to the other side of the walk "to comply with the law regarding such matters." Signs placed between the sidewalks and roadbeds were condemned for "destroy-

"Looking Down Eastern Approach, Mohawk Trail, Berkshire Hills," n.d. Postcard.

ing the beauty of the streets." [32] When the LHA did not have jurisdiction or laws on its side, members often took matters into their own hands. Summer resident Mrs. Herbert Parsons paid a landlord the rental fees for a billboard she disdained and immediately had it removed.[33]

Burgeoning tourism created situations that the LHA took in hand in its role as steward of community behavior. Men and boys providing valet service to motorists at the Red Lion Inn waited for customers across the way, by the Soldiers' Monument, public property maintained by the LHA. Concern was raised that the valets were defacing the turf and, in their hanging about, engaging in "general vandalism," and the LHA persuaded selectmen to put a stop to the practice. During the summer, visitors began traveling to the village by trolley to use the tennis courts and recreational grounds. Irate members pushed for signs to be posted that the facilities were exclusively for Stockbridge residents.[34]

One potentially threatening addition to Main Street was the Austen Riggs Foundation. The physician Austen Fox Riggs had become interested in psychology and psychiatry while he was recuperating from tuberculosis at his home in Stockbridge and, in 1913, founded the Stockbridge Institute for the Study and Treatment of Psychoneuroses, a voluntary-admittance facility. In the early days, patients would arrive by horse and buggy and board in the

"Austen Riggs Foundation – Offices – Stockbridge," n.d. Postcard.

village, but as more clients requested treatment, Riggs considered establishing a permanent residential facility.[35] The LHA took up "the question of the proposed Institute," and in 1919, the Austen Riggs Foundation moved into a remodeled house on Main Street.[36] Ten years later, as the Austen Riggs Center, the expanded facility moved to a property on Main Street, located on the site where Jonathan Edwards conceived some of his most famous works. The new building conformed to the village's standards of propriety so seamlessly that visitors rarely distinguished the campus from the residential neighborhood.[37]

The Laurel Hill Association would witness more change in the decades to come. Already, many cottagers were reducing their operating expenses by selling or donating large parcels of scenic acreage to state and charitable organizations. Although the village population steadily decreased, many of the affluent residents remained, and in 1921, Stockbridge could claim the title of "wealthiest town per capita in Massachusetts."[38] That year, The Trustees of Public Reservations transferred responsibility for Monument Mountain to the LHA. Members became the stewards of one of the Berkshires' most revered landscapes. During their first year of stewardship, the LHA reported on

"From the summit of Monument Mountain, looking North, Stockbridge," 1860–1930. Library of Congress Prints and Photographs Division.

maintenance efforts: cleaning and recutting the memorial rock, clearing paths and brush, posting directional signs, and disposing of rubbish left behind by crowds of picnicking automobile tourists.[39] The new charge not only broadened the association's responsibilities, but also kept members abreast of the growing threat tourism posed to the landscape they held so dear.

"Golf links by the Housatonic, Stockbridge," c. 1905–1915. Library of Congress Prints and Photographs Division.

SIX

PLANNING FOR POSTERITY

As it took on additional landscape stewardship, the LHA also became increasingly involved in planning issues created by the automobile. By the 1920s, villages in rural areas were overwhelmed by traffic, unsightly signs, and roadside businesses catering to auto tourists. Touted as "one large park" and "a motorman's paradise," the Berkshires had established itself as a destination, and Stockbridge was often a highlight of the trip.[1] The LHA had already taken a stand against billboards, hotdog stands, and camp-motels. Now it looked beyond Main Street to address difficult environmental problems, including pollution along the Housatonic and the growing number of dumpsites throughout the town. Zoning was presented as a means of comprehensively addressing all such issues.

Many LHA members first learned about zoning from a pamphlet issued in 1925 by the Massachusetts Federation of Planning Boards. Zoning, it explained, is constitutionally sound, and the health risks of choosing not to zone a municipality are rife. A comparison of zoning laws that applied to tenement houses, factories, and public buildings with those enforced on towns showed that in both cases, health and safety motivate the regulations. However, it warned, "when cities grow without plan, their constituent districts tend to change in character. Single houses give way to apartment houses; residential districts are insidiously invaded by business and manufacturing."[2] The rhetoric of the planning profession stoked the fears of a receptive audience, including LHA members. Another bulletin, *Planning Boards and Their Work,* touted zoning for protecting homes and preserving property values, declaring that towns should safeguard themselves through "eternal vigilance against encroachments in the form of billboards, shacks and similar nuisances."[3] This was exactly the support the LHA was looking for.

As the LHA considered these ideas, it made its own decisions on recreational zoning. In 1924 the executive officers voted to lease the meadows bequeathed by Emily Tuckerman to the privately owned Stockbridge Golf Club, retaining its right to trim trees on the property. The swath of meadowland was developed into a significant recreational facility. At the same time, the LHA kept an eye on its public land, attending to maintenance of Monument Mountain, the improvement of its Hickey Trail, and clearing brush and stumps along the road near the picnic grove. The committee overseeing public reservations put forward the idea of raising additional funds to purchase lands adjoining Monument Mountain with the intention of stimulating interest in the Berkshires, inspiring owners to bequeath property, and creating a permanent endowment for "improvement and development of the Monument Mountain Reservation."[4]

•

After the war, the Casino had begun a slow decline and by 1926 could no longer support itself. The Casino Association president hoped that the LHA might agree to lease the facility and serve as custodians, but after reviewing the matter, the association decided against taking on an additional public property.[5] Its fate in limbo, the Casino nevertheless hosted the year's annual Stockbridge Exhibition, with more than 140 artworks.[6] The event was supported by Grand Central Art Galleries, founded in New York in 1923 by Stockbridge's Walter Leighton Clark and his friend John Singer Sargent to provide exhibition opportunities for notable American artists. A significant celebration of American art, the exhibi-

Berkshire Playhouse, n.d. Postcard.

tion contributed to the village's growing reputation as a center for the humanities. Sculptures by the renowned locals Daniel Chester French and his daughter, Margaret French Cresson, added to the allure. Stockbridge was developing an economy based not only on its scenic beauty but also on its cultural value.

The worsening financial situation of the Casino Association came to the attention of Walter Clark, who with Austen Riggs and Daniel Chester French founded the Three Arts Society to continue the tradition of art exhibitions and the promotion of music and theater. At the same time, Mabel Choate, owner of her family's summer cottage, Naumkeag, felt it was urgent to save the abandoned Rev. John Sergeant house from demolition. An active philanthropist and preservationist, she believed the village's oldest house belonged on Main Street, as a historic house museum, and in 1927 purchased the Casino for the site. Choate sold the Casino building for a dollar to the Three Arts Society, who moved it to land they acquired on East Main Street at the foot of Yale Hill. After its first performance in 1928, the Berkshire Playhouse soon became famous for summer theater.[7]

While the Three Arts Society was prospering under its own management, Mabel Choate became the steward of two significant Stockbridge properties. Her ideas about the Mission House were informed by her friendship with the noted landscape architect Fletcher Steele, whom she had hired to design a garden at Naumkeag. Guided by Steele, Choate spent three years working on the

Mission House and outbuildings. Photo by Paul Weber. SUNY ESF College Archives.

restoration and preservation of the Mission House. After the house was carefully disassembled and reconstructed on the Main Street property, Steele sited outbuildings and designed colonial-inspired gardens and grounds. Choate guided its furnishing with Sergeant-era pieces, and the Mission House museum opened in 1930. Together, over three decades of collaboration, Choate and Steele would transform the landscape of Naumkeag, which, while retaining elements of its Victorian origins, evolved into an iconic modern garden, arguably the first in America.[8] The Mission House was donated to The Trustees of Reservations in 1948, and Choate bequeathed Naumkeag to the Trustees, ensuring her enduring legacy of preservation in the Berkshires.

•

As Main Streets throughout the nation acquired electric street lights, trolleys, and telephone lines, the Laurel Hill Association acted as a public voice and exemplar, sometimes to avert such modernization. Now the association had gained not only prestige and financial power, but also the authority that came from experience. The "Laurel Hill Spirit" was credited for keeping several attempts to modernize Main Street at bay through "neighborly action in the face of encroachments . . . upon the common heritage of natural beauty and civic order."[9]

The Laurel Hill Association also showed its spirit by looking after the Housatonic, a river W. E. B. Du Bois would describe as "the natural great highway of this valley."[10] Since the turn of the century, the LHA had warned against dumping rubbish into the river, and in 1922 a river fund was put under its jurisdiction.[11] In 1927 the association established a committee charged with maintaining the river, but despite efforts to clean it from the Hopkins Mill to the Sedgwick place, the following year they pronounced the Housatonic "a menace to the health of the community."[12] Over the next few years, more than a thousand dollars was invested in the cleanup effort.

Du Bois shared the association's frustration over the state of the river. A decade earlier he had published his autobiography, *Darkwater,* in which he recalled growing up near a river "that was golden because of the woolen and paper waste that soiled it."[13] In a speech to the alumni of his Great Barrington high school in the summer of 1930, he bemoaned the degradation of the Housatonic with "filth and refuse" and advocated for restoring "its ancient beauty." The Berkshires had turned away from a natural asset that other cities embraced to their advantage, as Cambridge had the Charles River. Du Bois offered "a little inquiry into the meaning of life in this valley," but his words were meaningless in the face of the industries fueling the region.[14] The Laurel Hill Association might clear its section of the Housatonic of debris and rubbish, but within a few years the General Electric plant in Pittsfield was dumping PCBs into the river.

At the 1931 Anniversary Day celebration, LHA president William Penn Cresson reluctantly acknowledged a change in focus for the association. The LHA could now only labor "to keep the town what it is—I may say—what it was." The automobile had become a national force, and the organization would attempt to preserve the village from its destructive effects. Stockbridge, "like all the more advanced communities in America is now more concerned in prying off the defacing 'improvements' which directly or indirectly the devastating advance of the automobile has foisted upon us, than in any more constructive task." At this point, the hope was to get unwanted vehicles, "notably the lumbering truck and the dingy caravan of the tourist lizzies," out of Stockbridge.[15] Maintaining the village's nineteenth-century form, character, and clientele—putting "aesthetics" before "commerce"—was now the LHA's mission.

Over the previous two decades Stockbridge residents had witnessed a gradual increase in traffic into the village, but now the congestion had become more than a nuisance. Main Street was at the crossroads of all east–west and north–south traffic moving through the southern part of the state. When commercial trucking further jammed roadways, hotel guests began to complain. Property values dropped along the noisiest section of Main Street, an area that had been one of the town center's most expensive locations. To address a growing problem, the LHA took up the concept of zoning first broached five years earlier. Corresponding with a state planning consultant, members received information on how to create a comprehensive zoning scheme and establish a town planning board. In 1932 a planning committee was appointed at town meeting in the hope of solving traffic problems and related issues.

That summer the LHA learned of a major threat to the "the identity of Stockbridge": state officials hoped to widen Main Street into a four-lane highway.[16] Native son Rep. Allen Treadway contacted the governor, and over the next two years the planning committee hired an engineer to create a zoning plan and a lawyer to draft a set of protective bylaws. Private subscriptions provided funds for the committee's operating budget and consultant fees. The effort was successful in persuading state officials not to widen Stockbridge's main artery.

As they confronted the invasive highway project, the association also accepted its largest gift of land—230 acres including the ground under Laura's Tower, a metal lookout erected by the LHA in 1931. A gift to the town from Lydia C. R. Sedgwick in honor of her husband, the property would become known as the Sedgwick Reservation. At the annual meeting on September 1, the LHA assigned a committee to keep the grounds in "rustic condition and the paths maintained."[17] The association became the steward of its own

Main Street crossroads, n.d. Postcard.

trail system at a time when the village seemed most vulnerable to encroaching development.

In February 1934 the citizens of Stockbridge passed the town's first zoning bylaws, drafted with direct input from the Laurel Hill Association, and elected five residents—all active members of the LHA—to serve on the new official town planning board. Regulations reinforced the pre-automobile character of the town. The center of the village, of primary concern, was zoned "residence," with a single block zoned for "business or shopping and marketing." Permits were required for restaurants, gift shops, tea rooms, newsstands, barber shops, hand laundries, boarding houses, hotels, funeral homes, hospitals, and sanitariums, as well as roadside refreshment stands, theaters, and movie houses. Tubercular camps and building uses "harmful to public morals" were prohibited.[18] No signs for lodging or other advertisements were allowed unless goods could be purchased on the premises (in that case, signs were restricted to two square feet). The zoning bylaws gave the LHA the agency to ensure the comprehensive protection and preservation of the town's physical character and community life.

The planning board was also charged with executing much more significant tasks of managing local development. These included "matters having to do with routes of travel, parks and playgrounds, opening of new streets, applications for permits from power lines and transportation lines, local building permits and studies of growth."[19] The community victory over the expansion of Main Street energized residents in defending the aesthetics and identity of their village. Now they began lobbying the state for a bypass. The Laurel Hill Association Anniversary Day keynote speaker of 1933 put it this way: "When a village continues to throw open its main street to through traffic, it is not only an anachronism—that village is doomed."

•

By the mid-1930s, the LHA faced the ironic challenge of trying to maintain Stockbridge's identity as a quintessential small, highly cultured New England village while the town's economy depended on auto tourism, with its increased traffic and crowds of transient visitors who threatened the very characteristics that attracted them. In the summer of 1935, an article on the Berkshires in the *New York Times* Resorts section reported on the upcoming Symphonic Festival to be held at Interlaken, which promised to "become an annual event of the same importance . . . as the Salzburg festival . . . has become to the musical world of Europe." The "flowering" of musical development was "part of a spreading interest in the arts evident in . . . these hills." Drama, painting, sculpture—all were "important in the Summer life." Gardening, too, was a major interest. And, "characteristic of many of the Summer colonists' enterprises [was] the effort to make them in some way enhance the region's charm." That year the Lenox Garden Club was offering cash prizes for "the best kept dooryards and front gardens."[20]

The Laurel Hill Association sought to maintain Stockbridge's aura of refinement, but the social picture was changing, as more middle- and working-class people could afford to travel by car. As one Anniversary Day speaker argued, "Our objection is not with the people who stay at the large summer hotels, it's the damned tourists" who sped through town, left trash in the parks, and encouraged roadside development like hotdog stands, camp-cottages, and gas stations. "The primary blame for this state of affairs," he insisted, "rests with Henry Ford and the mass production of low-priced automobiles."[21] Residents feared that Stockbridge would become a Coney Island when further expansion of the New York highways made the town more accessible.

In addition to traffic, crowds, and shifts in the social landscape, the LHA had to confront a serious threat to the natural landscape: the elm bark beetle. In 1928, when the *Berkshire Eagle* had announced the potential threat of a "Dutch Blight" migrating to the United States, it seemed a distant possibility. By 1942, however, several Stockbridge trees had died of the disease, and the LHA formed a special committee to report on infected elms. After learning of a ravaged tree on the golf links, the association brought in a Lenox horticulturist to investigate. At the September annual meeting, he announced that a USDA inspector had found diseased trees in a survey of Berkshire County. The only solution was to remove them. Although the town was responsible for managing the epidemic, the LHA acted quickly to try to save Stockbridge's trees. During an October 1948 meeting the association moved to create a town Dutch Elm Disease Authority. In the meantime its own special committee worked to "insure an aggressive campaign against the disease" with the help of town funding. Nevertheless, the arboreal affliction had soon become part of life in Stockbridge. The LHA recommended mapping the locations of diseased trees, the removal of which would be required by March 1, 1949.[22]

In the mid-forties, when the LHA first began fighting Dutch elm disease in earnest, its improvement campaign included three other initiatives: assisting in efforts to protect the Stockbridge Bowl, to purify the Housatonic, and to monitor trucks on major streets. Members were already witnessing the threat to their beloved Bowl. Roadways around the lake were widened, destroying the mature stands of trees that had lined them. Now that visitors avoided the polluted Housatonic, the Bowl saw bathing and boating traffic like never before. By the end of World War II, there were more than a hundred properties on the water and plans for two new lakeside developments. Community members began to worry that the Bowl would suffer the fate of Pittsfield's Pontoosuc Lake, now overdeveloped and its natural edges destroyed.

In 1946 the Reverend Dr. Anson Phelps Stokes, whose father had built Shadow Brook, founded the Stockbridge Bowl Protective Association to save "the most beautiful lake in the Berkshires" from "commercialism and spoliation."[23] The group planned to use regulatory controls to slow development, protect the Bowl from recreational overuse and environmental damage, and manage visual impact of buildings through landscaping and restricting paint colors to neutral tones.[24] Much of the program mirrored LHA efforts: enforcement of town zoning, planting trees and shrubs, and preventing commercial logging. The LHA contributed to the Stockbridge Bowl Association's purchase of a wooded island in the lake, a "conservation measure to protect the beauty of the bowl."[25] Discussions ensued about managing industry and tourism to encourage economic development while protecting natural areas from the effects of growth.

By the late 1940s, the LHA was guiding the town in regulatory planning at the county level to help manage the blooming tourist economy. Through the efforts of the South Berkshire Protective Committee, a regional preservation group, Stockbridge kept the hope of a village bypass alive and led the charge to divert traffic from regional roads.[26] Petitions were circulated and sent to the governor. Local legislators joined the crusade, and discussions with representatives from the Massachusetts Department of Public Works and the state Division of

Highways went on for years. Despite these efforts, Stockbridge residents faced a host of issues that would prevent them from securing a bypass.

This generation was no longer moved by the rallying cry that kept the trolley off Main Street. Summer residents did not come forward with funds to cover the costly endeavor—upwards of one million dollars. And because the state, rather than a private railway company, was behind the project, officials had to consider the interests of surrounding towns: traffic diverted around Stockbridge would have to go somewhere else. Further complicating matters was the lack of agreement on where the bypass would go. In a region with steep grade changes, routing it was difficult, and everyone involved realized that property values would plummet wherever the bypass was put. In the end, the state stalled the project, both because Stockbridge's bypass was not essential to military transfer—a priority since World War II —and because New York State was planning to build a connector section to its new Thruway, which would run through the Berkshires.

The lack of consensus among Stockbridge voters about the bypass reflects the struggles of a town that was slowly becoming more democratic as its middle class expanded, the wealthy became less affluent, and town government gained power. By the 1950s, the town managed most of the village center landscape as well as the municipal infrastructure of Glendale and Interlaken, the two other villages comprising the Town of Stockbridge. The elite no longer had the means or power to protect the central village, and only year-round residents could vote on town issues. The LHA continued its involvement with development issues, however, now working with selectmen and the town planning board. In 1953 they met to discuss a protective bylaw that would ban billboards from toll roads and limit the number and size of gas stations, and committed the association to clarifying the issues to community members and helping to maintain the effectiveness of the bylaws. Two years later, LHA members attended a Berkshire planning conference and returned with ideas for implementing coordinated regional planning among several towns, arguing that such cooperation was vital to sustain the area's value as an attractive destination.[27]

In spring 1955 the street-widening issue was reignited. The state highway department proposed widening South Street, as state Route 7, to four lanes where it intersected with Main Street at the Red Lion Inn. To many residents this was tantamount to running a four-lane highway into the center of town, already a congested space. This time, however, the debate involved all voting residents of the town, which gave voice to those in the more commercial villages of Glendale and Interlaken. Because summer "colonists" could not vote, their power was limited to lobbying year-round residents.

The Laurel Hill Association took action, this time with its denunciation of the project an official position of the organization. Uniting with the plan-

South Street at the Red Lion Inn and Fountain Park, n.d. Postcard.

ning board, they wrote letters to the governor, the district legislator, and former residents who might have some influence (including the Sedgwick clan). Some argued the traffic congestion issues, others the aesthetic and environmental concerns (the plan called for destruction of several mature elms). Some businesses supported the project, in the hope of attracting more customers, but the LHA argued that other towns with highways running through them had not experienced sharp increases in business—and the real loss would be the business of "desirable summer visitors."[28]

Alice McBurney Riggs, wife of Dr. Austen Riggs, expressed a core belief of the village improvement movement: that Stockbridge would no longer reflect American values if it lost its small-town aesthetics. She declared that Stockbridge had survived past encroachments and successfully adapted to pressures for building and infrastructure development because of its "inherent character." The town stood for "community interests, and . . . remained a sanctuary of beauty and refreshment." Not only did these "add material values, but they are essential ones to civilization as Americans believe in it."[29]

The selectmen, however, and other citizens, particularly those in Glendale and Interlaken, had reason to consider the benefits of the widening project. The proposed infrastructural changes would rebuild a section of town road badly in need of repair at no cost to the taxpayers. Since the selectmen had to answer every year for tax rate increases and bills for other municipal projects, state ownership of these improvements was welcome. When the LHA renewed lobbying for a bypass, property owners with adjacent land judged the widening as favorable to a loss in real estate value.[30]

Soon the entire county was involved in the village's battle. One regional press editorial described Stockbridge as a "town that resisted trolley cars half a century ago, fought a twenty-year battle for a Route 102 by-pass, and has always guarded its virtue with a fierce civic pride." But its opposition was "quaint at best or eccentric at worst—about what you'd expect from an ultra-conservative town that is more preoccupied with the past than the future." Another writer argued that the town's long history of fighting "trolley cars, truck traffic and other twentieth-century manifestations of 'progress,' is also the county's most charming and well-preserved community."[31] One Pittsfield resident remarked that Stockbridge sat "at a crossroads" reflecting countywide issues—"the problem of adapting country villages to vehicles they were never made for, of staking out living areas in a countryside increasingly laced by traffic."[32] Those most opposed to the widening, the planning board and the LHA, insisted that building a highway through its center would destroy the town's essential character. Did the town want to be "turned into a way-station on a naked express-way with all the resulting danger to our children" or would it "prefer to retain the character of the town as a residential area," attractive to both residents and "tourists who come to stay?"[33]

A special town meeting was called on May 21, 1955, to vote on the widening and designation of South Street as a section of state Route 7. The Laurel Hill Association's active lobbying of voters proved successful when the measure failed to pass, 121 to 46. Almost immediately, however, a vocal group of citizens protested the vote, claiming that the LHA and planning board had misrepresented the issues and clouded the discussion with their narrow interests. A month later, another vote was called. This time voting was by secret ballot and a greater number of voters came from Glendale and Interlaken, "two sections," one reporter stated, "that have never been much impressed by the arguments of the preservationists in the main village." The widening project passed, 147 to 70.[34] Incensed by the reversal, the Laurel Hill Association blamed the "so-called opposition" for stoking "the emotions of the Glendale element, who turned out en-masse for the fireworks." In the LHA president's view, town meetings were "senseless" and reasoning with the community fruitless. The only hope of preventing the widening was to fight the state highway department directly.[35]

The battle against the South Street project revealed the weakening influence of the Laurel Hill Association. In the past, working with those in power and relying on expert guidance had consistently brought the LHA its desired results, but now the players had changed. Control over the town's landscape resided more with the state than with local citizenry: professional planners were the expert consultants. At this point the LHA was publicly perceived as a conservative and narrow-minded band of preservationists standing in the way of progress.

Nevertheless the LHA was successful in lobbying for a compromise. Through private meetings with local public officials, the group gained assurances that existing landscape elements—public amenities that the LHA had installed and still maintained—would be considered. South Street would not become a four-lane road. The Cat and Dog Fountain near the Red Lion Inn would remain, along with several trees slated for removal. Despite its waning power in the public eye, the LHA maintained its role as village elders, responsible for protecting and caring for the character of Stockbridge.

The association invited Charles W. Eliot II to deliver the keynote speech at Anniversary Day in 1955. Nephew of the esteemed landscape architect responsible for the founding of The Trustees of Reservations, Eliot had served first as director of the National Capital Park and Planning Commission developing the National Mall and later as director of the National Resources Planning Board. In his speech, "Planning in Stockbridge," Eliot urged the association to "act now to preserve the beauty of the area" by developing a survey and general plan for the town in preparation for the Massachusetts toll highway expected to be completed within the next two years.[36]

Afterward, the LHA decided to direct "an active campaign to interest the Selectmen and other Stockbridge groups in the general subject" of planning. To this end, members called on heads of local organizations and business owners to discuss surveying the town's assets and liabilities—the first step toward establishing a regional planning commission. Members attended the recent convention of the Massachusetts Federation of Planning Boards, and the association hosted a screening of *The City,* a film produced for the American Institute of Planners that had been shown at the 1939 New York World's Fair as part of the "City of Tomorrow" exhibit. Scripted by Lewis Mumford, with a score by Aaron Copland, the film had a simple message for the LHA: modern life and its industry, automobiles, and sprawling infrastructure would destroy places like Stockbridge unless planners stepped in to save them.[37]

AFTERWORD

In October 1953, Norman Rockwell decided to spend the winter in Stockbridge. His wife Mary had been seeking treatment for alcoholism at the Austen Riggs Center since 1951. During her stay at the facility, Rockwell was pursuing his own outpatient treatment with Erik Erikson, the renowned German psychoanalyst who had joined the Riggs staff in 1951. For an illustrator of American small-town life, Stockbridge had the requisite charm, architectural features, and cast of characters. The town was in the throes of reorienting its economy around middle-class auto tourism, but it also attracted residents and visitors who enjoyed the arts. Perhaps most important for Rockwell, Stockbridge was a place where a famous person with mental health issues could lead a fairly normal daily life. The Riggs Center looked like the other stately homes on Main Street, and its patients were fully integrated into the community. Rockwell could see a psychiatrist and trust that his therapy, as well as wife's condition, would be handled with discretion. By the following spring, the Rockwells had moved from their home in Arlington, Vermont, and become permanent residents of Stockbridge.

When Rockwell settled in his new hometown he was a household name, having painted more than three hundred covers for the *Saturday Evening Post*. In 1957 he undertook a project for Hallmark, painting Stockbridge's Main Street for a Christmas card. He made little progress on the picture, however, and that winter it remained on an easel in his studio. During the spring of 1958, Herbert R. Mayes, editor of *Good Housekeeping,* saw the sketched canvas and asked to buy rights for one-time use in the magazine's Christmas issue, but nothing came of the offer, and the painting remained unfinished for nearly a decade.

Rockwell was at the height of his career in 1959, when Edward R. Murrow asked to interview him for his popular television series *Person to Person*. During each episode, Murrow would sit in the studio and with his viewers watch a screen as the camera first showed the outside of the subject's home and then faded into a living room scene. With Norman Rockwell, however, Murrow began with a journey down Main Street. Spotlights moved with the camera along the snowy streetscape, past the white clapboard Old Corner House (where the first Rockwell Museum would be established ten years later), the stately public library, and the eighteenth-century Red Lion Inn as Murrow narrated: "Main Street in Stockbridge . . . It's here, in the bank, the grocery store, the gas station, the school and of course the village barber shop that Norman Rockwell finds the people he paints into situations that so many of us find so realistic and intimate."[1]

Rockwell finally finished his painting of Main Street for the December 1967 issue of *McCall's*. In *Home for Christmas* he presented Stockbridge as the physical and cultural embodiment of the American small town. As the magazine circulated to millions of readers, a print of the painting appeared on newsstands and in mailboxes, and town residents gathered for Rockwell to sign their copies. Former visitors wrote fan letters thanking him for bringing back memories of time spent in Stockbridge, "looking at the very scene [he] so vividly portrayed." The painting quickly became part of the collective consciousness of white middle America.[2]

The iconic image of Stockbridge that Norman Rockwell created, and the increasing pride residents felt through his influence, helped the town resist not only typical 1960s development, but also its counterculture. *Home for Christmas* did not include The Back Room, commonly known as Alice's Restaurant, the subject of Arlo Guthrie's debut album, released earlier that year. The title song, like Rockwell's painting, was based on real places and people. The son of Woody Guthrie, Arlo knew the town well. Alice Brock ran a café at 40 Main Street. The hillside where he and his friend threw rubbish is in a residential area just beyond the village center. It was Chief Obanhein, Officer Obie to locals, who arrested him. Despite the immense popularity of the album, however, the town effectively

Norman Rockwell, *Home for Christmas*. From *McCall's*, December 1, 1967.

erased evidence of its counterculture, choosing not to build a tourist economy based on the folksong or to establish itself as a pilgrimage site.

By the late 1960s, residents were confident that the negative side of tourism could be controlled, largely because the community had curbed development using regulatory measures backed by the state's regional planning and conservation expertise. In 1968, when a developer considered buying the Old Corner House for a retail site, a group of citizens established the Stockbridge Historical Society to save it. Private subscriptions were obtained to preserve the house and convert it into a local museum. The LHA donated a thousand dollars toward its purchase. Norman Rockwell contributed a few of his paintings, and the Old Corner House soon became known as the first museum of his work.[3] *Home for Christmas,* exhibited a year after the museum's founding, shows the Old Corner House on the far left, Rockwell's first studio in the center near the lighted Christmas tree, and his home on the far right.

The LHA continued to play a prominent role in maintaining its vision for Main Street. In the late 1970s, the association responded to complaints about large crowds of young people gathering at the Music Inn, a rock concert venue. In partnership with the Berkshire Association of Concerned Citizens, the LHA posted a public letter inviting townspeople to attend a "Special Town Meeting to show our Selectmen whether it's the Rockwell Stockbridge or the Rock promoter's Stockbridge that we, the citizens, wish to preserve and encourage." Motorcycles and cars with no mufflers only invited "reckless activity" and had no place in town, they argued. "Give our Selectmen the clear message: 'the tranquil and safe Stockbridge portrayed so simply but elegantly by Norman Rockwell is not just a romantic ideal—it is and must be a reality.'"[4] Two months later, the Music Inn had lost its license and shut down.

In 1975 the town officially endorsed Rockwell's vision by publishing its annual report with a photo of the artist on the cover, brush in hand, posed in front of a local map. Although dismissed during his lifetime by art critics, Rockwell's work was being reconsidered toward the end of the century, and planning began for a contemporary museum, outside of the historic village. In 1993 a new facility designed by the renowned New York architect Robert A. M. Stern opened on thirty-six acres overlooking the Housatonic River Valley. Rockwell's South Street studio was moved to the site and restored to its 1960 appearance.

Every December since 1989 the town has transformed itself into the iconic village during "Stockbridge Main Street at Christmas," a winter weekend festival sponsored by the chamber of commerce and the Norman Rockwell Museum. Visitors enjoy "walking through the painting" for two hours. Main Street is closed to traffic and vintage cars are arranged on the street, but otherwise little needs to be done. The buildings are all there, and if it snows the effect is magical.

Home for Christmas remains a significant part of the town's identity, emblematic of a preservation ethic that dates back to the late 1900s, when the Laurel Hill Association first began protecting the scenery it had created.

Main Street in Stockbridge welcomes visitors looking for a sense of the past. Among them are members of the Stockbridge-Munsee Band of the Mohican Nation, who have created virtual and printed walking tours of Mohican historical sites along Main Street. The Stockbridge-Munsee Historical Committee's *Brief History* includes a photograph of Rockwell's unpublished painting *Sergeant and Konkapot* with the caption, "In 1738, the Mohicans gave John Sergeant permission to start a mission in the village."[5]

NOTES

Records of the LHA are held in the Laurel Hill Association Collection (LHAC) of the Stockbridge Library Museum & Archives, organized by series: Subject Files; Administrative Files; Minutes and Meetings; Books; Financial Records; Maps; and Plot Plans.

INTRODUCTION

1. [David D. Field and Chester Dewey], *A History of the County of Berkshire, Massachusetts; in Two Parts* (Pittsfield: Printed by Samuel W. Bush, 1829), 269.
2. Ibid.
3. R. H. Howard and Henry E. Crocker, eds., *A History of New England, Containing Descriptive and Historical Sketches,* vol. 1 (Boston: Crocker, 1880).

1. A MISSION IN WESTERN MASSACHUSETTS

1. Nathaniel Goodwin described Jones as "a well-read antiquarian and genealogist" and used her book in his own study. See Nathaniel Goodwin, *Genealogical Notes, or Contributions to the Family History of Some of the First Settlers of Connecticut and Massachusetts* (Hartford, CT: F. A. Brown, 1856), 136.
2. Electa F. Jones, *Stockbridge, Past and Present; or, Records of an Old Mission Station* (Springfield, MA: Samuel Bowles, 1854), introduction. The history became an important source for successive historians tracing the early origins of the Mohicans.
3. The copy Jones had on hand came from New York, without its first and last leaf, but excerpts from the complete version had been published in Timothy Dwight's *Travels; in New-England and New-York: in Four Volumes* (1821). Jones notes that Dwight, a former president of Yale, owned the only known perfect copy, now in the collection of the Massachusetts Historical Society. The MHS published "Extract from an Indian History" in 1804. Neither Dwight nor the MHS identified Aupaumut as the author. See *Collections of the Massachusetts Historical Society,* ser. 1, vol. 9 (1804), 99–102.
4. He may have been baptized by Jonathan Edwards. Rachel Wheeler, "Hendrick Aupaumut: Christian-Mahican Prophet," *Journal of the Early Republic* 25, no. 2 (Summer 2005): 194.

5. Jones, *Stockbridge, Past and Present*, 15.

6. Ibid., 14. John Warner Barber, *Massachusetts Historical Collections, Being a General Collection of Interesting Facts, Traditions, Biographical Sketches, Anecdotes &c, relating to the History and Antiquities of Every Town in Massachusetts* (Worcester, MA: Dorr, Howland, 1839), 95.

7. Jones, *Stockbridge, Past and Present*, 10.

8. Ibid., 27.

9. Rev. Samuel Hopkins, *Historical Memoirs, Relating to the Housatonic Indians* (1753; repr., New York: William Abbatt, 1911).

10. Dorothy Davids, "A Brief History of the Mohican Nation Stockbridge-Munsee Band," Stockbridge-Munsee Historical Committee, Arvid E. Miller Memorial Library Museum, Bowler, WI (2001; rev. 2004), 3; PDF available at https://www.mohican.com/services/cultural-services/ under Arvid E. Miller/Museum tab.

11. Hopkins, *Historical Memoirs*, 16–17. The board was an agency of the Church of England's Society for the Propagation of the Gospel in Foreign Parts.

12. Ibid., 15. Rev. David D. Field notes that Konkapot's "desire to be instructed in Christianity had led on, more than any other circumstance, to the establishment of the mission." See [David D. Field and Chester Dewey], *A History of the County of Berkshire, Massachusetts; in Two Parts* (Pittsfield: Printed by Samuel W. Bush, 1829), 239.

13. Wheeler, "Hendrick Aupaumut," 193.

14. Hopkins, *Historical Memoirs*, 17–18.

15. Ibid., 22.

16. Ibid., 30–31.

17. Barber, *Massachusetts Historical Collections*, 97.

18. Hopkins, *Historical Memoirs*, 49.

19. Belcher also realized that moving the Indians to a central location would benefit the missionaries. Barber, *Massachusetts Historical Collections*, 95.

20. [Field and Dewey], *History of the County of Berkshire*, 251.

21. Jones, *Stockbridge, Past and Present*, 58–59.

22. Nathaniel Hillyer Egleston, "A New England Village," *Harper's New Monthly Magazine* 43 (November 1871): 818.

23. David D. Field, *An Historical Sketch of the Congregational Church, Stockbridge* (Stockbridge: The Church, 1888), 8.

24. Lion G. Miles, "The Red Man Dispossessed: The Williams Family and the Alienation of Indian Land in Stockbridge, Massachusetts, 1736–1818," *New England Quarterly* 67, no. 1 (March 1994): 58.

25. Electa would go on to marry Col. Mark Hopkins. Among their grandchildren were Mark Hopkins, a future president of Williams College, and Mary Hopkins, founder of the Laurel Hill Association.

26. Williams Special Collections, available online at: https://specialcollections.williams.edu/williams-history/biographies/ephraim-williams-jr/. A second will, dated 1755, specified "a free school in the township west of Fort Massachusetts," the future site of Williamstown.

27. [Field and Dewey], *History of the County of Berkshire*, 246; Barber, *Massachusetts Historical Collections*, 95.

28. Jones, *Stockbridge, Past and Present*, 156.

29. Douglas L. Winiarski, "Jonathan Edwards, Enthusiast? Radical Revivalism and the Great Awakening in the Connecticut Valley," *Church History* 74, no. 4 (December 2005): 683–739. Edwards's most popular book, a best seller known as *The Life of David Brainerd*, was inspired by the work of his student, who died of tuberculosis while living in the Edwardses'

home. Jonathan Edwards, *An Account of the Life of the Late Reverend Mr. David Brainerd* (Boston, 1749). Joseph Conforti, "Jonathan Edwards's Most Popular Work: 'The Life of David Brainerd' and 19th Century Evangelical Culture," *Church History* (Cambridge University Press) 54, no. 2 (June 1985): 188–201. The minister's decision to carry on the mission at Stockbridge may also have been influenced by Brainerd, as well as by the opportunity to escape from the limelight and devote more time to his writings.

30. Egleston, "A New England Village," 822.
31. *Concerning the End for Which God Created the World* and *Concerning the Nature of True Virtue* were published posthumously in 1765.
32. Jonathan Edwards Jr., designated the keeper of family papers, was a linguist fluent in the Mohican language and president of Union College. Jones, *Stockbridge, Past and Present,* includes notes and translations from his *Observations on the Language of the Muhhekaneew Indians* (New Haven, 1787).
33. Jones, *Stockbridge, Past and Present,* 230.
34. Ibid., 168.
35. National Archives, FoundersOnline, https://founders.archives.gov/?q=Aupaumut&s=111 1311111&sa=&r=3&sr=.
36. Wheeler, "Hendrick Aupaumut," 195.
37. Lion G. Miles, "Anna Bingham: From the Red Lion Inn to the Supreme Court," *New England Quarterly* 69, no. 2 (June 1996): 287–99.
38. Davids, "Brief History," 3.
39. [Field and Dewey], *History of the County of Berkshire,* 257.

2. THE SEDGWICKS OF STOCKBRIDGE

1. Samuel Gray Ward (1817–1907), a poet, author, and part-time transcendentalist, cofounded the Metropolitan Museum of Art. Highwood (1845) was his first home in the Stockbridge region. In 1876 the architect Charles McKim designed Ward's second summer residence, Oakwood, on the Stockbridge Bowl property later occupied by Anson Phelps Stokes's Shadow Brook.
2. Samuel Longfellow, ed., *Life of Henry Wadsworth Longfellow,* vol. 2 (Boston: Ticknor, 1886), 121. Mrs. Sedgwick was Susan Livingston Ridley, Theodore Sedgwick Jr.'s wife.
3. Ben Z. Rose, "Stockbridge Slave Mum Bett and Her Appeal for Freedom," *Walloomsack Review* 16 (Autumn 2015): 18–28; Arthur Zilversmit, "Mumbet: Folklore and Fact," *Berkshire History* 1 (Spring 1971): 2–14.
4. Thomas J. Campanella, *Republic of Shade: New England and the American Elm* (New Haven: Yale University Press, 2003), 71.
5. Anna Bingham hosted the 1793 annual meeting of the organization, known as the Berkshire Republican Library, at her home. Harry Miller Lydenberg, "The Berkshire Republican Library at Stockbridge, 1794–1818," *Proceedings of the American Antiquarian Society* 50 (1941): 145, 156.
6. [David D. Field and Chester Dewey], *A History of the County of Berkshire, Massachusetts; in Two Parts* (Pittsfield: Samuel W. Bush, 1829), 10.
7. Ibid., 273–75.
8. *The Marble Border of Western New England: Its Geology and Marble Development in the Present Century,* Papers and Proceedings of the Middlebury Historical Society, vol. 1, pt. 2 (1885), 19, 31–33.
9. Sixty-four free Black people lived in Stockbridge by 1790. *Heads of Families at the First Census of the United States Taken in the Year 1790* (Washington, DC: GPO, 1908), 9. Negro

Swamp was later known as Muddy Brook Swamp. Rick Wilcox, "Bidwell Lore—The House of Elizabeth Freeman," 2022, https://www.bidwellhousemuseum.org/blog/2023 /09/05, and "Bidwell Lore—The Division of Land Around Lake Agawam," ibid., 2023/04/04/.

10. Freeman's likeness as an older woman is preserved in a 3 x 2″ miniature watercolor portrait on ivory painted by Catharine's friend and sister-in-law Susan Livingston Ridley Sedgwick. Kerri Lee Alexander, "Elizabeth Freeman," National Women's History Museum, 2019, www.womenshistory.org/education-resources/biographies/elizabeth-freeman. Mary E. Dewey, ed., *Life and Letters of Catharine M. Sedgwick* (New York: Harper & Brothers, 1871), 42.

11. Dewey, ed., *Life and Letters,* 44, 59.

12. Ibid., 60.

13. Q. D. Leavis, *Fiction and the Reading Public* (1932; rpt., New York: Russell & Russell, 1965); Daniel Walker Howe, *The Unitarian Conscience: Harvard and Moral Philosophy, 1805–1861* (Cambridge: Harvard University Press, 1970); David J. Rothman, *The Discovery of the Asylum: Order and Disorder in the New Republic* (Boston: Little, Brown, 1971); Ronald G. Waters, *American Reformers, 1815–1860* (New York: Hill and Wang, 1978); Richard L. Bushman, *The Refinement of America: Persons, Houses, Cities* (New York: Knopf, 1992).

14. Hugh M. Flick, "Elkanah Watson's Activities on Behalf of Agriculture," *Agricultural History* 21, no. 4 (October 1947): 193–98. Elkanah Watson, *History of Agricultural Societies, on the Modern Berkshire System* (Albany, NY: D. Steele, 1820), 123.

15. Watson, *History of Agricultural Societies,* 125–28.

16. Flick, "Elkanah Watson's Activities," 94. In his 1820 book advertising the Berkshire system, Watson announced that agricultural societies existed in every county with the exception of Rhode Island, and also gave himself credit, in his subtitle, for establishing the State Board of Agriculture in Albany.

17. Richard D. Birdsall, "William Cullen Bryant and Catharine Sedgwick—Their Debt to Berkshire," *New England Quarterly* 28, no. 3 (September 1955): 349–71.

18. Dewey, ed., *Life and Letters,* 151.

19. Sedgwick's cousin was a descendent of Eunice Williams, known as the "Unredeemed Captive" in the 1704 Deerfield Massacre. Karen Woods Weierman, "Reading and Writing *Hope Leslie:* Catharine Maria Sedgwick's Indian 'Connections,'" *New England Quarterly* 75, no. 3 (September 2002): 415–43. Dewey, ed. *Life and Letters,* 129.

20. Authorized editions of the book were soon published abroad by John Miller of London. Miller issued her first four books: *A New-England Tale; Redwood, A Tale* (1824); *The Travellers: A Tale Designed for Young People* (1825), and *Hope Leslie; or Early Times in the Massachusetts* (1827). Unauthorized reprints of these, and later volumes, resulted in a broader readership in England than in America at midcentury. See Melissa J. Homestead, "American Novelist Catharine Sedgwick Negotiates British Copyright, 1822–57," *Yearbook of English Studies* 45 (2015): 196–215.

21. Dewey, ed., *Life and Letters,* 59.

22. Electa F. Jones, *Stockbridge, Past and Present; or, Records of an Old Mission Station* (Springfield, MA: Samuel Bowles, 1854), 211.

23. Established in 1792, the school was among the first to offer a substantial curriculum in addition to needlework and moral training. Pierce's Female Academy not only was considered the most esteemed institution of its type, but also benefited from its proximity to Litchfield Law School.

24. Following the deaths of his brother, John Sergeant Hopkins, and sister-in-law, Lucinda Hopkins, Archibald had taken on the responsibility of their orphaned children.

25. Huldah's name appeared in the commonplace book of classmate Louisa C. Lewis, written in 1817. Emily Noyes Vanderpoel, *Chronicles of a Pioneer School from 1792 to 1833, Being the History of Miss Sarah Pierce and Her Litchfield School* (Cambridge, MA: University Press, 1903), 446. She is also included in a "list of Julia Anna Shepard," dated October 1818. Emily Noyes Vanderpoel, *More Chronicles of a Pioneer School, from 1792 to 1833* (New York: Cadmus Book Shop, 1927), 21.

26. Vanderpoel, *Chronicles,* 259.

27. C. A. Weatherby, "Old-Time Connecticut Botanists and Their Herbaria," *Rhodora* 16, no. 185 (May 1914): 83–90.

28. Vanderpoel, *More Chronicles.*

29. Weierman, "Reading and Writing *Hope Leslie,*" 436–42.

30. Clark W. Bryan, ed., *The Book of Berkshire, Describing and Illustrating Its Hills and Homes* (Great Barrington: C. W. Bryan, 1886), 31.

31. Ibid., 74.

32. For a thorough account of Thomas Green Fessenden's stature as a promoter of tree planting, see Richard Ross Cloues, "Where Art Is Combined with Nature: Village Improvement in Nineteenth-Century New England," 3 vols. (PhD diss., Cornell University, 1987), 1:305–9, quot. 307.

33. "Ornamental Tree Society," *New England Farmer, and Gardener's Journal,* October 22, 1834, cited in Cloues, "Where Art Is Combined with Nature," 1:319–20; *Gardener's Magazine* [London] 11 (April 1835): 207 and (June 1835): 280–84.

34. Theodore Sedgwick Jr., *An Address, Delivered before the Berkshire Agricultural Society, October 7, 1830* (Pittsfield: Printed by Phinehas Allen & Son, 1830).

35. David Schuyler, *Apostle of Taste: Andrew Jackson Downing, 1815–1852* (Amherst: LALH, 2015), 30.

36. Rev. Frank H. Kasson, "Mark Hopkins," *New England Magazine* 3 (September 1890): 3–9; Albert C. Sewall, *Life of Prof. Albert Hopkins* (New York: Anson D. F. Randolph, 1870), 118.

37. N. P. Willis, "Pedlar Karl," *New Monthly Magazine* 42 (December 1834), 446–47.

38. Catharine Sedgwick, *Hope Leslie; or Early Times in the Massachusetts,* 2 vols. (New York, 1827), 1:140.

39. G. W. Curtis et al., *Homes of American Authors* (New York: G. P. Putnam, 1853), 171.

40. Dewey, ed., *Life and Letters,* 225–26.

41. Constitution of the Laurel Hill Association, c. 1900, LHAC.

42. Robert D. Birdsall, "Berkshire's Golden Age," *American Quarterly* 8, no. 4 (Winter 1956): 328.

43. Dewey, ed., *Life and Letters,* 227.

44. Catharine Sedgwick, *Letters from Abroad to Kindred at Home,* 2 vols. (New York: Harper & Brothers, 1841), 1:152, 231, 151, 170, 53, 41–42.

45. "Amid Summer Scenes," *New York Times,* June 21, 1914.

46. *The Berkshire Jubilee, celebrated at Pittsfield, Mass., August 22 and 23, 1844* (Albany: Weare C. Little; E. P. Little, Pittsfield, 1845), 39. Catharine Sedgwick is credited with changing the name of the Great Pond to The Bowl by translating the Mohican name, "Quit-chu-scook." Mrs. L. H. Sigourney, *Scenes in My Native Land* (Boston: James Munroe, 1845), 200–202.

47. *Berkshire Jubilee,* 144.

48. Ibid., 122–23.

49. William Cullen Bryant, "A New Park," *New York Evening Post,* July 3, 1844.

50. Schuyler, *Apostle of Taste,* 190–91.

51. A. J. Downing, "On Planting Shade-Trees" (November 1847), in *Rural Essays* (New York: G. P. Putnam, 1853), 300.

52. A. J. Downing, "Trees in Towns and Villages" (March 1847), ibid., 308. The Chelsea Ornamental Tree Society's plans for planting "the borders of all the streets and avenues" there are mentioned in "Ornamental Tree Fair," *Boston Evening Transcript,* May 21, 1850.

53. Dewey, ed., *Life and Letters,* 315–17; Fredrika Bremer and Adolph B. Benson, "Fredrika Bremer's Unpublished Letters to the Downings," *Scandinavian Studies and Notes* 11, no. 6 (1931): 187–205.

54. Joseph Edward Smith and Thomas Cushing, *History of Berkshire County, Massachusetts, with Biographical Sketches of Its Prominent Men,* vol. 2 (New York: J. B. Beers, 1885), 595.

55. Sarah Cabot Sedgwick and Christina Sedgwick Marquand, *Stockbridge, 1739–1939, A Chronicle* (Great Barrington: Printed by the Berkshire Courier, 1939), 137.

56. Joe Roman, "In Melville's Footsteps," *New York Times,* September 3, 2004.

57. Curtis et al., *Homes of American Authors,* 169–71.

3. THE LAUREL HILL ASSOCIATION

1. Electa F. Jones, *Stockbridge, Past and Present; or, Records of an Old Mission Station* (Springfield, MA: Samuel Bowles, 1854), 234–35.

2. "The Elm-Tree Association—Address by Rev. Orville Dewey, D.D.," *New York Times,* September 9, 1856.

3. No archives of the Elm Tree Association have survived. For more on Orville Dewey's effects on Sheffield and philosophies in relation to village improvement, see Thomas J. Campanella, *Republic of Shade: New England and the American Elm* (New Haven: Yale University Press, 2003), 83–98.

4. Walter Prichard Eaton, "Second Fiddle?," *Berkshire County Eagle,* August 13, 1941.

5. Looking back on a decade of work, the LHA described the condition of the village and its subsequent improvements. Minutes, August 10, 1864, 13.

6. Sarah Cabot Sedgwick and Christina Sedgwick Marquand, *Stockbridge, 1739–1939, A Chronicle* (Great Barrington: Printed by the Berkshire Courier, 1939), 244.

7. Margaret French Cresson, *The Laurel Hill Association, 1853–1953* (Pittsfield: Eagle Printing & Binding, 1953), 9.

8. The statute went into effect May 10, 1853. "An Act to Regulate Agricultural, Horticultural and Ornamental Tree Associations," *Acts and Resolves Passed by the Federal Court of Massachusetts* (Boston: White & Potter, 1853), chap. 312, 782–83.

9. "John Z. Goodrich," *Boston Globe,* November 30, 1883.

10. Minutes, August 24, 1853, 1.

11. "Letter from Kossuth to the Ladies of Stockbridge," *New-York Daily Times,* January 19, 1852.

12. Minutes, August 24, 1853, 1.

13. Ibid., September 3, 1853, 2–3.

14. E. W. Canning, "Town of Stockbridge," in Thomas Cushing, ed., *History of Berkshire County, Massachusetts, with Biographical Sketches of Its Prominent Men,* 2 vols. (New York: J. B. Beers, 1885), 2:589–90.

15. A. J. Downing, *Rural Essays* (New York: George P. Putnam, 1853), 330–31; Minutes, May 15, 1854, 3.

16. Ibid., 4.

17. Ibid., September 4, 1854, 5.

18. Stephen E. Burrall, *An Address Delivered before the Laurel Hill Association of Stockbridge, Mass., August 22, 1855* (Boston: T. R. Marvin, 1855); quot. from Downing, *Rural Essays,* 301.

19. LHA Annual Report, 1855. See Richard Ross Cloues, "Where Art Is Combined with

Nature: Village Improvement in Nineteenth-Century New England," 3 vols. (PhD diss., Cornell University, 1987), 2:505.

20. Minutes, June–August, 1856, 6–7.
21. Ibid.
22. Cloues, "Where Art Is Combined with Nature," 2:501–2.
23. Minutes, October 5, 1857, 8.
24. LHA Annual Report, 1857; Cloues, "Where Art Is Combined with Nature," 2:499.
25. In 1858 the holiday was a tribute to "Stockbridge boy" Cyrus W. Field, the leading force behind the completion of the first transatlantic telegraph cable just a week earlier. This "great event of the age" was recognized with cheers for Field, "multiplied to three times three, and closed by the timely discharge of a cannon." Minutes, August 11, 1858, 8.
26. "The Laurel Hill Anniversary," *Berkshire County Eagle,* August 11, 1859.
27. "Housatonic," *Berkshire County Eagle,* August 18, 1859.
28. Minutes, August 13, 1963; August 10, 1864, 11–13.
29. Ibid., August 10, 1864, 13.
30. Ibid., August 8, 1866, 15.
31. Egleston was minister of Stockbridge Congregational Church 1861–69 and an association officer. Ibid., July 23, 1866, 14.
32. Ibid.
33. Cloues, "Where Art Is Combined with Nature," 1:41, 611.
34. Minutes, July 29, 1867, 17.

4. IMPROVING THE NATION'S VILLAGES BY EXAMPLE

1. "Local Intelligence," *Pittsfield Sun,* August 13, 1868.
2. Birdsey Grant Northrop, "How to Make a Town Beautiful," *Hearth and Home* 1, no. 2 (January 2, 1869), 28.
3. Ibid.
4. Minutes, August 18, 1869, 23. Northrop continued to write and lecture into the 1880s, and his work inspired a young Black legislator from Texas, Robert Lloyd Smith, to found the nation's first known Black village improvement society in 1889. Recognizing the need to focus on economic reform projects aimed at confronting poverty among Black farmers, the group reorganized as the Farmers' Improvement Society. Before its gradual decline in the 1920s, the FIS had more than 21,000 members in chapters across Texas, Oklahoma, and Arkansas. Purvis Carter, "Robert L. Smith: The Farmers' Improvement Society, A Self-Help Movement in Texas," *Negro History Bulletin* 29, no. 8 (Fall 1966): 175–76, 190–91; Robert Carroll, *Robert Lloyd Smith and the Farmers' Improvement Society of Texas* (master's thesis, Baylor University, 1974).
5. Minutes, August 18, 1869, 23.
6. Ibid., August 4, 1870, 26.
7. "The Edwards Clan," *New York Times,* September 5, 1870.
8. Minutes, August 7, 1871, 29.
9. Richard Ross Cloues, "Where Art Is Combined with Nature: Village Improvement in Nineteenth-Century New England," 3 vols. (PhD diss., Cornell University, 1987), 2:612–13.
10. Minutes, September 6, 1869, 24.
11. The Edwards Monument, a column of pink granite, was erected in 1873. Margaret French Cresson, *The Laurel Hill Association, 1853–1953* (Pittsfield: Eagle Printing & Binding, 1953), 41.
12. Minutes, September 4, 1871, 29.

13. "Rev. N. H. Egleston Dies. At One Time Chief of the U.S. Bureau of Forestry," *New York Times,* August 12, 1912.

14. Nathaniel Hillyer Egleston, "A New England Village," *Harper's New Monthly Magazine* 43 (November 1871): 829.

15. Cloues, "Where Art Is Combined with Nature," 1:47.

16. Minutes, August 27, 1873, 33.

17. Ibid., August 26, 1874, 34. Brigadier General Samuel Chapman Armstrong (1834–1893), a graduate of Williams College, was married to Emma Dean Walker of Stockbridge. In 1868 he founded Hampton Normal and Agricultural Institute to train Black teachers and began admitting Native Americans ten years later. Booker T. Washington attended the school and, with Armstrong's encouragement, went on to found Tuskegee Institute. See *Encyclopedia Virginia* at https://encyclopediavirginia.org/entries/armstrong-samuel-chapman-1839-1893/.

18. George E. Waring, "Topics of the Time: Village Reform," *Scribner's Monthly* 14 (May 1877): 110.

19. George E. Waring, *Village Improvements and Farm Villages* (Boston: James R. Osgood, 1877), 20.

20. Minutes, August 25, 1875, 37.

21. Ibid., August 22, 1877, 40.

22. "Villages and Village Life," *Chicago Daily Tribune,* September 21, 1878.

23. Nathaniel Hillyer Egleston, *Villages and Village Life with Hints for Their Improvement* (New York: Harper & Brothers, 1878), 64. The book was reissued in 1884 in a revised edition under the title *The Home and Its Surroundings, or Villages and Village Life with Hints for Their Improvement.*

24. Ibid., 119, 133, 14–15.

25. Ibid., 58–59.

26. Minutes, April 8, 1878, 42–44.

27. Cresson, *Laurel Hill Association,* 43–46. A carved inscription on a stone at its base reads "The Burial Place of the Housatonic Indians, the Friends of our Fathers." Minutes, August 28, 1878, 45.

28. Minutes, August 27, 1879, 47.

29. "Stockbridge," *Pittsfield Sun,* September 3, 1879.

30. Rev. Jeremiah Slingerland, "The Stockbridge Indians, Their Fortunes and Wanderings," Anniversary Day address, 1879, LHAC.

31. "Stockbridge," *Pittsfield Sun.*

32. Minutes, October 7, 1878, 45; August 27, 1879, 48.

33. Ibid., October 5, 1880, 53.

34. Ibid.

35. "Sanitary Improvement," *New York Times,* July 8, 1882.

36. M. F. Sweetser, *New England: A Handbook for Travellers,* 6th ed. (Boston: Houghton, Osgood, 1879), 149.

37. LHA, *Town Report* (Great Barrington: Clark W. Bryan, 1884), LHAC.

38. "Stockbridge Notes," *Berkshire County Eagle,* March 13, 1884; Minutes, August 26, 1884, 64; *Berkshire County Eagle,* "New Livery and Blacksmith," April 17, 1884; H. M. Plunkett, "The Evolution of Beautiful Stockbridge," *New England Magazine* 25 (October 1901): 216.

39. Stockbridge Casino Company, Minutes, July 11, 1884, 31, Casino Company Records, Stockbridge Library Museum & Archives; "Arrivals at Stockbridge: Settling Down for the Summer—Opening of the Casino," *New York Times,* June 7, 1896.

40. Minutes, August 26, 1885, 69.

41. "Reclaiming Old Farms. The Summer Visitor and the Trolley, the Best Ever," *St. Albans [Vermont] Daily Messenger*, September 5, 1901; Nathalie Sedgwick Colby, *Remembering* (Boston: Little, Brown, 1938), 88.

42. Sarah Cabot Sedgwick and Christina Sedgwick Marquand, *Stockbridge, 1739–1939, A Chronicle* (Great Barrington: Printed by the Berkshire Courier, 1939), 238.

43. Anonymous review of *Lenox and the Berkshire Highlands* by R. De Witt Mallary, *Nation*, August 14, 1902, 137.

44. W. A. Croffut, *Boston Herald*, July 1882, quoted in Clark W. Bryan, *The Book of Berkshire . . . for the Season of 1887* (Great Barrington: Clark W. Bryan, 1887), 70; "A Cozy Berkshire Nook: Where Spring and Summer Come Hand in Hand. An Observer's Notes on the Restful Beauties of Stockbridge and the Berkshire Country," *New York Times*, July 5, 1886.

45. Colby, *Remembering*, 88; "Land Company in Stockbridge," *New York Times*, June 25, 1887.

46. "Autumn in Lovely Lenox," *Boston Evening Transcript*, September 22, 1894. Part of the Stokes estate encompassed the border between Lenox and Stockbridge, and over the years both villages claimed it as their own.

47. "A Great Farm Abandoned," *Indianapolis Journal*, July 5, 1903.

48. Carole Owens, *The Berkshire Cottages: A Vanishing Era* (Stockbridge: Cottage Press, 1984), 86–88, and *Pittsfield: Gem City in the Gilded Age* (Charleston, SC: History Press, 2007), 88.

49. Minutes, October 11–18, 1894, 93–95.

50. Cloues, "Where Art Is Combined with Nature," 1:49.

51. Goodrich's bequest included a parcel of land at the trailhead now known as Goodrich Park. The bridge is now the Goodrich Memorial Footbridge.

52. Minutes, April 1895, 96.

5. A TWENTIETH-CENTURY VILLAGE

1. Mary Caroline Robbins, "The Art of Public Improvement," *Atlantic Monthly*, December 1896; "Park-Making as a National Art," *Atlantic Monthly*, January 1897; "Village Improvement Societies," *Atlantic Monthly*, February 1897, 113.

2. "Pioneer of Improvers. Stockbridge's Society Has a Bright Record. How the Battle for Village Beauty Was Won by a Brave Woman," *Boston Daily Globe*, November 19, 1899.

3. Mira Lloyd Dock, "Forestry and Village Improvement," *Women in Professions, Being the Professional Section of the International Congress of Women*, London, July 1899 (London: T. Fisher Unwin, 1900), 159–60.

4. Mira Lloyd Dock, "Parks, Forests and Improvement Work," lecture, Arundell Club, Baltimore, January 21, 1903, Dock Family Papers, Pennsylvania Historical Commission.

5. Jessie M. Good, "Village Improvement Associations and Kindred Topics," *Chautauquan*, December 1900, 317, and *Village Improvement: Examples of the Work Accomplished by Improvement Associations [Extracts from a Series of Articles Published in HOW TO GROW FLOWERS, Springfield, Ohio]*, undated pamphlet, box 20, Charles Mulford Robinson Collection, Frances Loeb Library, Harvard Graduate School of Design.

6. By 1904 the American League for Civic Improvement had merged with the American Park and Outdoor Art Association as the American Civic Association. Richard Ross Cloues, "Where Art Is Combined with Nature: Village Improvement in Nineteenth-Century New England," 3 vols. (PhD diss., Cornell University, 1987), 3:1065–66.

7. Charles Mulford Robinson, *The Improvement of Towns and Cities, Or, The Practical Basis of Civic Aesthetics* (New York: G. P. Putnam's Sons, 1901).

8. "Plans for a Year of Active Work," *Home and Flowers* (Springfield, OH), October 1901, 12.

9. Sylvester Baxter, "The Beautifying of Village and Town," *Century Magazine*, April 1902,

849, 844; Charles Zueblin, "Civic Progress: A Decade of Civic Improvement," *Chautauquan,* November 1902, 174, 177.

10. "The Berkshire Trolley Line," *New York Times,* March 3, 1901; "For a Trolley Line in the Berkshires," *New York Times,* January 27, 1901.

11. Howard, Rev. R. H., and Henry Crocker, *A History of New England Containing Historical and Descriptive Sketches of the Counties, Cities and Principal Towns of the Six New England States, Vol. I: Massachusetts, Connecticut, Rhode Island* (Boston: Crocker, 1880), 105.

12. Colby's speech is quoted in "A Fight for an Avenue," *New York Times,* September 29, 1901.

13. Ibid.

14. According to his obituary, "Mr. Field built his first trolley car at his home in Stockbridge, and it was exhibited there in August, 1880." "Stephen D. Field, Car Pioneer, Dead," *New York Times,* May 19, 1913.

15. Minutes, September 10, 1905, 117.

16. Minutes, June 4, 1906, 118.

17. The funding also ensured that the trolley's electric lines would be placed underground. "The Facts in the Case," document signed by the Society for the Protection of the Highways of Stockbridge, LHAC.

18. *Stockbridge Town Report,* 1890 (Pittsfield: Sun Printing Company, 1891), LHAC.

19. Minutes, July 6, 1908, 120.

20. Roy Stone, comp., *State Laws relating to the Management of Roads Enacted in 1888–'93,* vol. 1 (Washington, DC: U.S. Department of Agriculture, Office of Road Inquiry, 1894), 53–54.

21. George A. Perkins, "By Improving the Roads," *Boston Daily Globe,* August 3, 1902.

22. "The Most Popular Automobile Touring Season of the Year Is at Hand. Attractive Trip, Covering Seven Days, Passes through the Heart of the Catskills, Skirts the Adirondacks, and Traverses the Green Mountains and the Berkshires—Uniform Good Roads Through Greatest Part of Mileage," *New York Times,* September 4, 1910; "A Cozy Berkshire Nook. Where Spring and Summer Come Hand in Hand. An Observer's Notes on the Restful Beauties of Stockbridge and the Berkshire Country," *New York Times,* July 5, 1886.

23. "Report of the Meeting of the Executive Committee of the Laurel Hill Association Held at the Casino in Stockbridge, Mass.," June 5, 1913. Dr. H. C. Haven presiding.

24. *Stockbridge,* February 1914, 8–9, LHAC.

25. Elizabeth Bullard to Frederick Law Olmsted Jr., September 25, 1913, Olmsted Associates Records, Job Files 1863–1971, File 5929, Library of Congress. Bernhard Hoffmann, a Cornell University graduate trained in electrical engineering, considered himself a summer resident but was born in Stockbridge.

26. Bernhard Hoffmann to Frederick Law Olmsted Jr., October 7, 1913, Olmsted Associates Records, Job Files 1863–1971, File 5929, Library of Congress. When Hoffmann moved from Stockbridge to Santa Barbara in 1919, he brought the tenets of the LHA with him. His first major community project, the restoration of the historic adobe "Casa de La Guerra," marked the beginning of a campaign to remake the city. Hoffmann became chair of the Plans and Community Planting Branch of the Arts Association, through which he established city zoning laws, and after the devastating earthquake of 1926, used his power to rebuild Santa Barbara as a "city in Spain." Hoffmann was later dubbed the "father of architectural planning in Santa Barbara" for his many contributions to the city. See Kurt G. F. Helfrich, "Site Work 4: Plaza de la Guerra Reconsidered—The History of a Public Space," in Patrick O'Dowd et al., *Plaza de la Guerra Reconsidered, Exhibition and Symposium* (Santa Barbara: Santa Barbara Trust for Historic Preservation, 2002), 11–14; Michael Redmon, "Bernhard Hoffmann, The Father of Architectural Planning in Santa Barbara," *Santa Barbara Independent,* May 1, 2014.

27. "A Report on the Improvement of the Town of Stockbridge by Harold Hill Blossom for Olmsted Brothers Landscape Architects," *Stockbridge,* Special Supplement, March 1, 1914, 3–15.

28. Harold Hill Blossom, "Andrew Jackson Downing: Landscape Architect," *American Magazine of Art* 8, no. 7 (May 1917): 263–68. Bernhard Hoffman to H. H. Blossom, November 14, 1917, image 50 of Olmsted Associates Records: Job Files, 1863–1971; Files; 5929; Laurel Hill Association; Town improvement; Stockbridge, Mass., 1913–1917, available at loc.gov/item/mss5257103537.

29. Hoffman to Blossom, ibid.

30. *Twenty-Second Annual Report of the Massachusetts Highway Commission* (Boston: Wright & Potter, 1915), 14.

31. "New Motor Route from Sea to Hills," *Boston Globe,* May 23, 1915.

32. Minutes, July 1, 1915, 127.

33. "Huge Billboard Removed," *Boston Daily Globe,* August 30, 1915.

34. Minutes, May 4, 1916, 128–29; June 2, 1916, 129.

35. Sarah Cabot Sedgwick and Christina Sedgwick Marquand, *Stockbridge, 1739–1939, A Chronicle* (Great Barrington: Printed by the Berkshire Courier, 1939), 270–71.

36. Minutes, August 7, 1919, 136.

37. Sedgwick and Marquand, *Stockbridge,* 275.

38. According to U.S. census records, Stockbridge's year-round population decreased from 2,132 in 1900 to 1,762 by 1930. Mrs. Andrew Carnegie's estate was valued at $261,825 (over $4.5 million today). Many of her neighbors owned properties worth $100,000 (over $1.5 million today). "Stockbridge Is Richest," *New York Times,* September 4, 1921.

39. *Thirty-First Annual Report of The Trustees of Public Reservations,* 1921; Minutes, May 6, 1921, 139. Ten years later, the LHA returned full responsibility for the property to the state.

6. PLANNING FOR POSTERITY

1. Warren James Belasco, *Americans on the Road: From Autocamp to Motel, 1910–1945* (Cambridge: MIT Press, 1979), 7. See also James R. Ackerman, "American Promotional Road Mapping in the Twentieth Century," *Cartography and Geographic Information Science* 23, no. 3 (2002): 181.

2. George C. Whipple, *Zoning and Health,* Massachusetts Federation of Planning Boards, Special Bulletin no. 1, Boston, March 31, 1925, 10.

3. Edward T. Hartman, *Planning Boards and Their Work,* Massachusetts Federation of Planning Boards, Special Bulletin no. 1, revised, Boston, March 1926, 3.

4. Minutes, June 5, 1924, 146; July 11, 1925, 149.

5. Ibid., June 26, 1926, 152.

6. "The Stockbridge Exhibition," *American Magazine of Art* 17, no. 11 (November 1926): 590–91.

7. Judy D. Dobbs et al., "Stockbridge Casino," National Register of Historic Places Inventory—Nomination Form, January 8, 1976.

8. Robin Karson, *A Genius for Place: American Landscapes of the Country Place Era* (Amherst: University of Massachusetts Press in association with LALH, 2007), 327–54. For more on the Mission House project, see Karson, *Fletcher Steele, Landscape Architect: An Account of the Gardenmaker's Life, 1885–1971* (Amherst: LALH, 2003), 116–19.

9. President's Report, 1928, LHAC.

10. W. E. B. Du Bois, "The Housatonic River," July 21, 1930, W. E. B. Du Bois Papers (MS

312), Special Collections and University Archives, University of Massachusetts Amherst Libraries.

11. Minutes, May 5, 1902, 109; May 4, 1922, 142.

12. Minutes, June 19, 1928, 159; September 6, 1928, 161; September 5, 1929, 163–64.

13. W. E. B. Du Bois, *Darkwater: Voices from Within the Veil* (New York: Harcourt, Brace and Howe, 1920), 10.

14. Du Bois, "Housatonic River."

15. W. P. Cresson, untitled introductory remarks, Seventy-Eighth Laurel Hill Association Anniversary Day, 1931, LHAC.

16. Allen T. Treadway to Rev. G. G. Merrill, Acting President of the Laurel Hill Association, August 30, 1932, LAHC.

17. Minutes, September 1, 1932, 171.

18. In addition, perhaps to avoid developments in other towns, the bylaws specifically prohibited tanneries, junk yards, automobile dismantling yards, bottling works, bulk stations for storage of explosives, and steam laundries. *By-Laws of the Town of Stockbridge,* Rewrite of July 27, 1933, LHAC.

19. Letter from Mr. E. C. Wilcox to Miss E. M. Herlihy, Chairman of the State Planning Board, Commonwealth of Massachusetts, January 18, 1936, LHAC.

20. "Berkshires Live Anew. Old Colonists' Love of the Hills Is Shown in the Spread of Cultural Projects," *New York Times,* July 28, 1935.

21. *Berkshire Evening Eagle*, September 10, 1937. The speaker was the landscape architect Edward F. Belches.

22. "Dutch Blight Is Feared as Menace to U.S. Elm," *Berkshire Eagle,* December 28, 1928; Minutes, November 20, 1942, 27; August 18, 1944, 46; October 2, 1947, 62; January 21, 1949, 77; October 19, 1951, 97–98.

23. "Club Set to 'Save' Stockbridge Bowl," *New York Times,* September 29, 1946.

24. "Protecting Stockbridge Bowl," *Berkshire Evening Eagle,* August 20, 1946.

25. Minutes, July 16, 1948, 70.

26. "Residents Studying Bypass Plans," *Berkshire Eagle,* October 16, 1939.

27. Minutes, March 18, 1955, 143.

28. Mrs. John Heather, "Laurel Hill Trustees Oppose Proposed South St. Road Job," *Berkshire Eagle,* May 13, 1955, and "Laurel Hill Wants By-Pass," *Berkshire Eagle,* May 19, 1955.

29. Alice McBurney Riggs, letter to the editor, *Berkshire Eagle,* May 17, 1955.

30. A. A. Michelson, "Stockbridge Re-Embattled," *Berkshire Eagle,* May 12, 1955.

31. Robert Linscott, "Stockbridge Voters Reflect an Outlook Too Rare in County," *Berkshire Eagle,* May 28, 1955; "In Brief," *Berkshire Eagle,* May 20, 1955.

32. A. G. Rud, "Stockbridge at the Crossroads," *Berkshire Eagle,* May 21, 1955.

33. Robert C. Alsop, "Wants Alternative," *Berkshire Eagle,* May 21, 1955.

34. "Stockbridge Reversal," *Berkshire Eagle,* June 25, 1955.

35. LHA President A. F. Forni to R. Minturn Sedgwick, June 27, 1955, LHAC.

36. "Laurel Hill Association Speaker to Talk on Town Planning," *Berkshire Evening Eagle,* August 24, 1955; "Laurel Hill Speaker Sees Need for Regional, Town Planning," *Berkshire Evening Eagle,* August 29, 1955.

37. Minutes, November 18, 1955, 147.

AFTERWORD

1. *Edward R. Murrow—The Best of "Person to Person,"* directed by Franklin J. Schaffner, DVD, 2006.

2. Correspondence files, Norman Rockwell Museum Archives, Stockbridge. The museum began tracking sales of Rockwell prints in the late 1990s.
3. The museum opened in 1969. "Presentation of the Story of the Stockbridge Corner House Corporation," document, LHAC.
4. Public letter to the Citizens of Stockbridge, June 1979, LHAC.
5. A PDF of *Footprints of Our Ancestors: Mohican History Walking Tour of Stockbridge* is available at https://www.nativeamericantrail.org/stockbridge-walking-tour/. Dorothy Davids, Stockbridge-Munsee Historical Committee, "A Brief History of the Mohican Nation Stockbridge-Munsee Band" (2001; rev. 2004), 3, Arvid E. Miller Memorial Library Museum, Bowler, WI. PDF available at https://www.mohican.com/services/cultural-services/ under Arvid E. Miller/Museum tab.

ACKNOWLEDGMENTS

Many years ago, when I was a graduate student at the University of Massachusetts Amherst, my interest in the Laurel Hill Association was first sparked by Jon Peterson's *The Birth of City Planning in the United States, 1840–1917*. Living less than sixty miles from Stockbridge, I was curious to see the the association's archives, and the trove of historical records—and engaged community members—I discovered led me to delving deeply into the landscape and planning history of this remarkable organization.

My guide in that early journey was Barbara Allen, now retired curator of the Stockbridge Library Museum & Archives. Barbara helped connect me with stories, resources, and people who would prove essential to my research.

The late Lion G. Miles, longtime Stockbridge resident and honorary member of the Stockbridge-Munsee band in Wisconsin, Bonney Hartley, tribal historic preservation manager for the Stockbridge-Munsee Mohican Nation, and Rick Wilcox, former Stockbridge police chief and dedicated local historian, provided insight into the history of Stockbridge's Indigenous people. Pat Flinn, recording secretary of the LHA since 1986, provided me with a room in her house and a tour of the association's properties. LHA board members Hilary and Phil Deely endorsed my project and spread the word.

Kind folks at the Red Lion Inn, the Mission House, Stockbridge Town Hall, the Sheffield Historical Society, and the Berkshire Athenaeum, Pittsfield's public library, welcomed me into their archives. During my time researching, I attended a Laurel Hill Association Anniversary Day, served as a volunteer tour guide at Naumkeag, and walked every foot of LHA's hiking trails. I am grateful to the citizens of Stockbridge for their warm welcome and genuine interest in this work.

For direction and support during early stages, I thank Max Page, Ethan Carr, and Patricia McGirr at UMass Amherst. Over the years, many generous people read drafts, listened to my stories, and showed enthusiasm for my work. In particular, I thank Annmarie Adams, Beth Belanger, Eric Bulson, Anna Creadick, Kate Fama, Shana Klein, Rosemary Krill, Erin Sweeney, and the late Boyd Zenner. Daniel Nadenicek at the College of Environment and Design of the University of Georgia provided valuable guidance as I developed the manuscript.

My work was supported by a National Endowment for the Humanities fellowship at the Winterthur Museum, Garden & Library and by the Massachusetts Foundation for the Humanities, the University of Massachusetts Amherst, Smith College, and Hobart and William Smith Colleges. Structured writing retreats hosted by Susan Pliner and the staff at the Center for Teaching and Learning at Hobart and William Smith provided space and time to write. Grants from the Norman Rockwell Museum, the Maine Women Writers Collection at the University of New England, the Texas Collection at Baylor University, and Archives & Special Collections at the University of Connecticut Library supported visits to their collections.

I am grateful to Robin Karson, executive director of the Library of American Landscape History, for her sincere interest in this book and dedication to its success. The essential contributions of Sarah Allaback, LALH senior manuscript editor, are nominally credited as coauthor. Sarah's skills are a unique treasure, and I want to express my deep gratitude to her here. Carol Betsch, LALH managing editor, brought invaluable editorial expertise to the project and gathered the wealth of historical photographs that bring the story to life. Joshua David Hall, assistant curator at the Stockbridge Library Museum & Archives, was generous in his enthusiasm and help with images. Mary Bellino created a top-tier index, catching errors along the way. Jonathan Lippincott designed a beautiful book.

I also want to acknowledge my late colleague, friend, and writing buddy, Cadence Joy Whittier, for many joyful and productive co-working sessions. I will always be grateful for that time together and the sincere interest she took in my work and career.

Finally, my deepest gratitude goes to my family—my husband, Dustin; my parents, Donna and Sudesh; and my brother, Vishal. Their love and support continue to sustain me.

INDEX